THE SINGING THING

G-5510

THE SINGING THING

A case for congregational song

John L. Bell

GIA PUBLICATIONS, INC.
CHICAGO

First published in North America by
GIA Publications, Inc.,
7404 S. Mason Ave., Chicago, IL 60638, USA.
www.giamusic.com
Exclusive North American distributor

ISBN 1-57999-100-9

Cover design © 2000 Graham Maule

Printed by Bell & Bain, Thornliebank, Glasgow, UK

Kyrie Eleison, p.31: melody © 1987 Dinah Reindorf;
arrangement © 1990 Iona Community

Alleluia, p.32: music by Norah Duncan IV, © GIA Publications, Inc.,
7404 S. Mason Ave., Chicago, IL 60638, USA.

Hymn lyrics *Though one with God* p.51-52 © The Iona Community

Extract from *He'll Have to Go*, p.74, by A. Allison & J. Allison,
© Campbell Connely Ltd.

All biblical quotations except where otherwise specified are from *The
Revised English Bible* © Oxford University Press and Cambridge
University Press, 1989

CONTENTS

INTRODUCTION

ACKNOWLEDGEMENT

As well as being indebted to innumerable and unnamable people whose experiences have informed and shaped this book, I wish to acknowledge my gratitude to the following:

Fr Michael Joncas for a thought-provoking lecture to hymn-writers which was the germ for the section 'The Ambiguity of Communication'.

Alison Adam, Graham Maule and Mairi Munro who read and commented on the first draft of the book.

Sandra Kramer of Wild Goose Publications who sensitively edited the rather crude manuscript which witnessed to the author's technological naivety.

If further and slightly more academic reading on issues of musical perception is sought, a very singular book is *Music, the Brain and Ecstasy* by Robert Jourdain, published 1997 by Avon Books, New York (ISBN 0 380 78209 X).

Fondly dedicated to
Marion Morton and Thomas C. Aitken
who told me I could not sing

Introduction

Comparatively few books have been written about women's mud wrestling...and this is not one of them. But this book is similar to those dealing with that exotic sport, in that there are not many in its field.

There are plenty of books – as there are courses – about vocal or choral technique, organ interpretation, hymnody and liturgy. But not much has been written which specifically addresses the practice of congregational song.

For this reason (you will be pleased to hear, dear reader) the present volume is the first of two books. This one deals with the *why*, the second will deal with the *how*.

But please do not feel cheated because you do not have in your hands the blueprint for turning the twenty people who attend your favoured mission hall into the congregational equivalent of the Mormon Tabernacle Choir. That will come. First it is important to get a handle on why we sing. For if we are going to encourage people to use their voices in worship there must be reasons as to why they sing, apart from obedience to the worship leader who announces the hymn number, and fear of the musician who glowers defiantly at the congregation.

This book is unapologetically anecdotal. It does not deal with musical theories; its raw material is the people of God with whom my colleagues and I have been privileged to work for the past 15 years in most parts of Britain and Ireland, and in every continent. Without them, whose experience and stories we draw on, neither this book nor their singing congregations would be possible.

John L. Bell
April 2000

SECTION ONE

Why do we sing?

But first of all, why you should not skip this section and read the next one instead.

It is probable that you think you know very well why you sing, and it may seem much more interesting to discover why a cousin, parent or spouse does not. Therefore head for Section B.

However, if we are at all interested in encouraging others to sing or improving the quality of their singing, we don't simply need to know why things go wrong, we need to be able to give good and persuasive arguments as to why things should go well.

Any musician, priest or minister who stands in front of a congregation and tells them to 'sing as if you mean it!' is on a hiding to nothing. People will sing well because they mean it. If they do not mean it, why should they fake it just to keep the leader happy?

So here are some persuasive reasons – ten or thereabouts – as to why people sing.

Some of the sections are bigger than others. This could indicate that some of the reasons are more complex than others. Or it could mean that the writer knows more about some than others. Both explanations are equally plausible.

1. Because we can

Greeks do it, freaks do it,
Nice young men who sell antiques do it.
Let's do it. Let's... (Noel Coward, adapted)

Like walking, swimming, snapping fingers, gargling, turning cartwheels and whistling in the dark, singing is a human potential.

The good news is that we do not need any equipment to do it, apart from ourselves. The bad news is that one in four people believe they can't. This book devotes a whole section to them and their plight. So we need not concentrate on the problematic side immediately.

Singing is a natural thing. A baby and its nursing mother do it unselfconsciously. The one goo-goos multisyllabic nonsense, while the other lah-lahs in the hope of soothing the crying one or encouraging sleep. Many people do it in the bath or shower either because they are flattered by the reverberant acoustic, or because they presume they cannot be heard when pelted by warm water.

Football supporters do it, especially when the home team needs a boost or the opposition needs to be discouraged. Teenagers do it when carried away by the all-round headphone sound which transports them from a dingy bus-shelter to the main stage at Glastonbury music festival.

And all of us, whatever our age, absent-mindedly hum or croon when knitting, fixing the car or trying to disguise the fact that we don't know what we are doing.

Singing is a natural thing – even more natural than turning cartwheels or swimming. These activities will probably be done irregularly if at all by the majority of adults, yet schools would be pilloried for not teaching physical education. We can sing at any hour of the day or night, but the educational emphasis on developing this potential is sadly lacking – at least in British schools.

This was not always the case. Until the 1960s class singing was the principal musical activity in schools. And county music festivals – let alone Mods or Eisteddfodau – had entrants from infants to sixth form. Indeed many church choirs of an earlier era were indebted to schools for developing a confidence in singing from which congregations benefited.

In the first half of the twentieth century, it was not just the renowned Welsh valleys or Hebridean islands which nurtured singers. Villages in Ayrshire, Northumberland and Norfolk could not only boast choirs in every congregation, but would often have a local choral society singing Mendelssohn's *Elijah* or Handel's *Messiah* from tonic sol-fa.

There was then a belief that everyone – or most people – could sing, and that singing was as much a manly as a womanly activity.

If that belief is in demise in Britain, it is not so elsewhere. Our neighbours in Eastern Europe, especially in Hungary, regard musical education of the young as an essential. The Kodaly and Orff methodologies aim to get children as young as four singing from sol-fa (sol-fege) notation, transferring to staff a few years later.

And in sub-Saharan Africa, singing in harmony is an everyday human activity. One only need remember news bulletins from South Africa during the apartheid era which showed footage of rallies or funeral processions during which there was unaccompanied community singing of immense passion and energy.

Indeed, there are choirs in Soweto which outstrip former British village choirs in their ability to learn Handel's *Messiah*, not from sol-fa notation but simply from memory.

On several occasions the author has had the privilege of working with people such as George Mxadana from South Africa, Sr Benedicta of the Holy Paraclete Order in Botswana, and Patrick Matsikinyiri of Zimbabwe, each of whom knows the three to five-part harmonies of hundreds of songs which they have learned by ingestion rather than by instruction.

When Sr Bene was asked to teach a song from her nation, she asked if we wanted the alto, bass, tenor or soprano first. After the four parts had been sung, Bene was asked how she had learned these, given that she did not read music.

'I learned them at home,' she replied. 'People sang all day. My mother sang the tune, my grandmother was alto, my father was tenor and my grandfather bass. So I just picked it up like that. Now when I'm in the convent and there are no men – which is most of the time – I just sing my father's or my grandfather's line.'

If this seems a million miles away from our present situation, it need not be so. For there was a time in Britain when not only did people believe in their voices, but they also evidently believed in their ability to instantly recall melodies and harmonies they had learned.

The proof is found in a diarist's account of something which happened in Edinburgh in 1582. John Durie, a reformer who had been living in exile on the Continent, returned to his native city. He docked at Leith and made his way to the Royal Mile. When he reached the Netherbow:

they took up the 124th Psalme, 'Now Israel May Say', etc., and sung in such a pleasant tune in four parts, known to the most part of the people, that coming up the street all bareheaded till they entered the Kirk, with such a great sound and majestie, that it moved both themselves and the huge multitude of the beholders...[1]

Singing is a natural activity, and peculiarly suited to humans. For while birds improvise melismatic lines, donkeys bray and hyenas laugh, only humans have the ability to ally words to melody and produce songs for a community to sing.

We sing because we can.

---

[1] Quoted in *Four Centuries of Psalmody* by Millar Patrick (Oxford UP, 1949)

2. To create identity

Scots, wha hae wi' Wallace bled,
Scots, wham Bruce has aften led,
Welcome to your gorry bed
or to victory.   (Robert Burns)

We cannot all speak together, but we can all sing together.

Anyone who has observed a congregation reading a liturgical prayer for the first time will know the truth of this. Worse still may be listening to a congregation which has been encouraged to 'read together the Old Testament lesson which comes from...'

Different people will read at different speeds; some will observe longer or shorter pauses at commas and semi-colons; some will stumble over unfamiliar words. The result is an unholy mêlée.

But we can all sing together. For music provides us with a regular pulse or beat, ensuring that we keep in time with each other. And even should we get a note wrong or mispronounce a word, we will soon rejoin the chorus of other people's voices. And because of this facility which singing offers, songs have for long been the means whereby people created or celebrated their identity.

The verse which begins this chapter is unlikely to be sung anywhere else but Scotland. The text and the tune are distinctly Scottish. It would not be appropriate for English mouths, the more so since it is from a diatribe against the 'auld enemy'.

Similarly the hymn *And did those feet in ancient time* (Jerusalem) rarely gets a singing in Wales, Ireland or Scotland. It is a distinctly English national text, and the singing of it will encourage a fervour in the hearts of Her Majesty's English subjects which cannot be emulated elsewhere in the United Kingdom.

One need only watch the Olympic crowds when the national anthems of the winning teams are being played to see how, in the middle of a huge and disparate gathering, unanimity prevails among the few for whom that tune and those words speak of home.

But, even within a nation, songs will create smaller regional or cultural identities.

If you walk through Central Station in Glasgow on a Saturday when Rangers and Celtic are playing at home, there will be two distinct groups of supporters who, even if team colours were forbidden, would be recognisable to each other by their favoured arias:

There's not a team like the Glasgow Rangers
versus
For it's a grand old team to play for

Should you go to a folk concert, watch how different people from within the one nation will join or refrain from the singing of different songs. While Lallans-speaking lowlanders would have little difficulty with the Robert Burns repertoire, they might be at sea with some Doric ballads from Aberdeenshire, and would probably stay silent as Gaelic speakers sang waulking songs from Barra or demonstrated nonsense-syllabled mouth music in the manner of their particular island. While everyone can sing, not everyone can sing everything.

The study of ethno-musicology has charted how different parts of the world have indigenous scales in which their peculiar melodies are written. Indeed, in parts of China there are specific combinations of sounds which are believed to have moral quality, as they signify good or evil. Some of these scales and some tunes from other cultures may be awkward for us to sing.

Not everyone hearing indigenous music in an Asian restaurant may feel able or keen to join in the chorus, such is the effect of quarter- and microtones on Western ears. It will be similarly awkward for Europeans to slur notes together as happens in some Indian ragas; and it would be well nigh impossible for British choral singers to feel comfortable with the ultra-close harmony of parallel seconds which Bulgarian women's choirs delight in, or to indulge themselves in the syncopated rhythms which typify Afro-American jazz and Gospel music.

Yet to people within these ethnic communities, what seems odd to us will be perfectly natural, and what seem to us to be perfectly good tunes may be considered banal and dull.

The singing of songs can be a tribal activity, and the Christian churches are not exempt from this. Put a random two thousand British Christians in one room and begin the introduction to:

And Can it Be
Ye Gates Lift Up Your Heads,
Faith of Our Fathers,
Just As I Am,
Majesty

and different sets of Methodist, Presbyterian Roman Catholic, Baptist or Charismatic hearts will swell as they discover that the band is playing their song.

More than ever before, the tribal factor is evident in contemporary commercial music. Indeed, one has difficulty in finding a blanket term for this entity. Pop and rock are now specialist rather than general categories. They take their place alongside rap, acid house, funk and a dozen others, all of which have their own devotees.

We sing and select music to express our group identity.

3. To express emotion

I sing because I'm happy,
I sing because I'm free.
If God can see the sparrow,
I know he's watchin' me. (Trad. spiritual)

When most people are asked why they sing, they respond subjectively. They will not talk immediately about fulfilling a human potential or expressing group solidarity. They will say something like:

'I sing because I feel happy.'

or

'I sing because it makes me feel good.'

Singing has undoubtedly something to do with the emotions, and whether singing makes us feel or feeling makes us sing is a chicken-and-egg argument. Sometimes we launch into a song because of the mood we are in and sometimes the very act of singing can lift us from carelessness to courage. That is why, in war and in training for war, every tribe and nation has had its battle-songs to boost the military morale.

This reflection or expression of emotion is, however, not just to do with the positive sides of our nature. We also sing or croon to muse over the troubled side of life, its disappointments, frustrations and pain. And that in itself can be therapeutic.

An elderly lady in Kilmarnock wrote recently of how she had to come to terms with a body which did not always work the way she wanted it to. Her antidote to that physical and psychological pain was song:

In my lowest moments I sometimes just begin to sing out loud, and I know that God hears me.

It is interesting to reflect on the spectrum of songs which we, in our daily lives, might employ to express or accompany the changes of mood during the day.

If we are feeling very happy – (and this, of course, will depend entirely on our musical predilections) – we may find ourselves singing:

Oh, what a beautiful morning!
or
I could have danced all night
or
I'm so glad, I'm so glad, I'm glad, I'm glad, I'm glad.

If we are in a middling emotional range, we might go for:

Summertime, and the living is easy
or
If I were a rich man
or
Michelle, ma belle.

If we are in the depths of despair, we might have recourse to Leonard Cohen, or we might turn on a country and western radio programme and hum along to lyrics which illustrate how dire life can be:

I went into my house and found
my wife had upped and gone,
and that my dog was dead
and that she'd trashed the telephone.
I found there was no whisky left
nor bullet in my gun.
So I sat right down and wrote me out
the lyrics of this song.

For some cultures, Afro-American in particular, it is not so much the text or tune which expresses emotion as the speed at which the song is sung.

In a seminar a number of years ago at the Greenbelt Festival at Castle Ashby, a black Gospel singer introduced a predominantly white audience to the styles of singing common in his church. He taught the audience a fast tune to the lyrics:

I'm satisfied with Jesus,
I'm satisfied with him.
His love for me will never die;
I'm satisfied with Jesus.

This, he said, would be accompanied by keyboards, drums, bass and guitar at Sunday morning worship. 'But if I go home,' he continued, 'and discover that someone I love dearly has just died, I will sing the same song, but in an entirely different way.' And then he began, in a mournful, plaintive voice, to let that song be suffused with grief and anguish.

I experienced the same potential in the music of the spirituals when I was asked to celebrate eucharist in a London prison. The congregation, mirroring the mix of the metropolitan prison population at large, had a high proportion of black inmates.

What, I thought, would be an appropriate *Kyrie* to sing during the eucharist?

Eventually I settled not on the classical penitential text, but on the simple three-note chorus of a spiritual which a generation of BBC viewers were introduced to as an entertainment song, courtesy of *The Black and White Minstrel Show*.

A profound sense of integrity, intentionality, prayer and the presence of God was felt as the prisoners began to sing ever so slowly:

It's me, it's me, O Lord,
standin' in the need of prayer.

It is interesting to reflect on whether most churches allow for the broad spectrum of emotion to be represented in their singing. Sometimes one gets the impression that charismatic congregations sing predominantly rousing praise choruses, that middle-of-the-road Anglican and Methodist churches favour bland but positive hymns, while Presbyterians and other Calvinists by style of singing, if not by subject-matter, inhabit the deserts of negativity and unhappiness.

It is the extremes – the acclamations of joy and the expressions of remorse, anger and sorrow – which deserve more attention.

With all respect to Genevan Psalmody and the 1650 Scottish Psalter, *All People That on Earth Do Dwell* does not often sound like the great exciting song of praise it should be. The guardians of metrical psalmody will probably either protest that singing exuberantly is not a cultural characteristic – 'We are not emotional people' – or claim that forced expressions of joy are more to do with entertainment than worship.

While the latter point may be true, the former has little foundation. We are all emotional people, but different people feel comfortable expressing different emotions.

Preachers know this when they try their hardest to speak of the gracious love of God, seeking out the lost, lifting the downhearted, bringing hope to the hopeless. At the church door they will find their hands courteously shaken as people walk into the open air.

But should they forsake gentle tones and a positive subject, and instead rant and rave about the depravity of humanity, raising and lowering their voice and beating the pulpit Bible into pulp, their hands will be tightly grasped as people (especially men) assure them of how blessed they were by the preaching.

The enthusiasm for the second type of sermon is as much evidence of the worshippers' being emotional as if they were to cry with joy and stretch their hands in the air, but few of the aficionados of doom and gloom would admit it.

There is a true sense in which we are in danger of seeing the depths of sorrow, anger and confusion lost from our singing. Those who favour bright choruses tend to shy away from reflecting the 'shadow' side of our emotional spectrum in song, perhaps because they think it is unchristian, or perhaps because they are afraid of aspects of their character yet to be offered to God. Those who favour more traditional hymns can be equally evasive of the depths, claiming that when we speak of that which is in the lower registers of our soul, it has to do with guilt. Nothing could be further from the truth, and anyone who wants to equate justifiable anger or intense frustration with guilt has simply not read the Gospel.

Some years ago I met a woman who had left Scotland in her teenage years to go on an eastern trail to India, Thailand and other exotic places. En route, she met a boy from a town in Michigan. They travelled together through New Zealand and Australia and eventually made their way back to his home town where they set up house together.

After a while she, who was a lapsed Roman Catholic, thought she would like to go to church. She went to a lively charismatic fellowship where she was converted and became a born-again Christian. She encouraged her partner to come and he underwent the same transformation. The church sang Hallelujah.

Soon afterwards, they decided to get married. The church was thrilled with the news. A year after their wedding she gave birth to a son, and the church could not contain its joy at how God had blessed this beautiful couple.

Two years later she had a miscarriage, and a year after that she had a stillborn child, and when these hard things happened to this fine young couple, no one from the church went near them, although some began to speculate openly that perhaps these mishaps were God's way of showing disapproval for the time they had lived out of wedlock.

When asked what had kept her in faith, for she was clearly a committed Christian, she replied:

'During the very dark days, I could not go to my church. I could not sing endless praise and worship songs, because they seemed to deny what I was going through. I would have been a hypocrite to do otherwise. So I stayed away from church, but I began to read my Bible. And I read for the first time in English the psalms I had learned as a child in Latin...words like *De profundis acclamavi...* (Out of the depths I call to you, O Lord.)

'I discovered phrases like,

How long, O Lord, will you forget me?
How long will you turn your face from me?

'And as I read such words, I realised that the psalms were saying to God what I needed to say. And that kept me in faith.'

There is a very true sense in which if we are not enabled to cry, 'How long?' we may never be able to shout 'Hallelujah'.

The music of the church has to embrace and express our whole emotional and spiritual spectrum. We have no right to expect country and western singers to do it for us.

4. To express words

Happy birthday to you,
happy birthday to you,
happy birthday dear N...
happy birthday to you! (anon)

Spoken it sounds banal. But put the universally known tune to it, and it comes alive, and even those who don't know a minim from a microwave will harmonise the last two bars. Music expresses words.

Equally revealing is a public reading of the text of arias and recitatives in Italian operas. The genius of Mozart and Verdi is not only that they wrote magnificent music, but that their music is able to disguise what is sometimes a banal text.

They were able to do this because they understood how music did not simply need to ally bland words to ineffectual melody. Music can also articulate words, flesh out their meaning, and provide a range of resonances through which people may understand the text.

It is instructive in this respect to look at the way in which simple liturgical texts have been set.

Kyrie Eleison (Lord, have mercy) is one of the oldest prayers of the Church. Thousands of composers have set it to music and each setting consciously or unconsciously interprets the simple text.

Here are three very different examples. The first is a meandering melody from the Greek Orthodox Church. It may be sung with some voices droning on the tonic.

The second is a brisk three-part setting from the Ukrainian Orthodox Church.

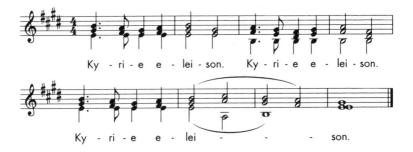

And the third was more recently written by a Ghanaian composer, Dinah Reindorf.

These are clearly very different. The first is mysterious, the second is joyful, the third is deep and penitential.

Each setting says something different about the simple prayer, *Kyrie Eleison*. The first evokes the unfathomable nature of God's mercy, the second evokes the generous and jubilant nature of God's mercy, the third marries the grace of God to the heartfelt penitence of the people.

The same contrast can be found in different *Hallelujahs*.

Here, for example, is a bright *Hallelujah* from an Afro-American musician in Detroit. It is a sheer delight to be in a congregation singing this in three parts at a wedding or festival mass.

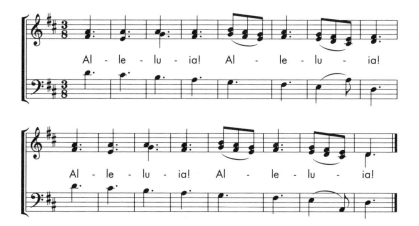

The second is much slower. It was transcribed from a Christian Aid video of a memorial service for victims of apartheid. While it was sung, the music leader, George Mxadana, sang a plaintive descant beneath which the congregation's *Alleluia* (Praise the Lord) expressed the worship of a people's sorrow.

There are, in secular and sacred music, melodies which perfectly fit the text with which they are associated. In the realm of twentieth-century standards, *Oh What a Beautiful Morning* and *Jingle Bells*

are two clear examples. There is no way that either of these tunes could turn a lively text into a dirge.

In the more classical repertoire, *When I am Laid in Earth* from Purcell's *Dido and Aeneas* is a perfect lament, while Verdi's setting of the *Dies Irae* in his *Requiem* bristles with tumult and foreboding, reminiscent of the Day of Wrath.

Hymns such as *Praise, My Soul, the King of Heaven*, and *All My Hope on God is Founded* (set respectively to the tunes *Praise My Soul* and *Michael*) are examples of happy marriages.

But it doesn't always work.

Take, for example, the text

For all the saints who from their labours rest.

There was a competition to find a tune for these words. Two distinguished composers made submissions. Ralph Vaughan Williams wrote the tune (*Sine Nomine*) which won. It is an ideal match, expressing dignity, gratitude and a sense of the ongoing life of the saints.

Charles Villiers Stanford also submitted a beautiful tune (*Engelberg*), but it was a pale if prestigious second in its ability to articulate the text.

There are also some unions of word and tune which, though popular, just don't seem to make it. An example of this might be

While humble shepherds watched their flocks
set to the tune *Windsor Old*:

The Scottish word 'dreich' best describes this limp and joyless melody which is totally inadequate to accompany a text about the announcement of such a stupendous event as the incarnation.

And then there are other marriages of tune and melody which are more contentious. Think, for a moment, of spending the evening in the quiet and intimate company of a trusted friend. You are going over what in each of your lives is important to you, talking about tender issues as well as fond memories. You perhaps make coffee or pour a glass of port. And, as the conversation continues, you turn on the radio for some appropriate background music.

Imagine how you would feel if from the speakers came blasting out a brass band playing:

It would be wholly inappropriate. You would want something which respected the intimacy of the evening, not something which jarred.

Now, the above tune, called *Converse* is popularly associated with the text

What a friend we have in Jesus

As you read that text, it is clear that the emotions and atmosphere evoked are compatible with a sensitive conversation with a trusted friend.

Have we trials and temptations?
Is there trouble anywhere?
or
Are we weak and heavy-laden,
cumbered with a load of care?

These are words of intimacy and vulnerability which do not deserve to be shouted triumphantly. They should be pondered over gently.

It was therefore interesting to discover that a helper in a home for the elderly in Glasgow had taken to singing this with her charges to the tune *Scarlet Ribbons*:

Here is a much more sensitive and appropriate match. Or is it?

Those who don't dispute that music expresses words, but who do feel aggrieved at the suggestion that *Converse* should be divorced from *What a Friend*, may be dealing with something entirely different which we will look at in the next chapter.

5. To revisit the past

Yesterday,
all my troubles seemed so far away;
now it looks as though they're here to stay.
Oh, I believe in yesterday. (Lennon & McCartney)

Songs, like smells, are highly evocative.

You can be sitting on the underground quietly minding your own business. Then someone sits down to your left and you discover that she or he is wearing the same perfume or aftershave which was the favourite of an old friend whom you haven't seen for a decade. Suddenly the person next to you becomes significant. The scent has invoked strong memories which will linger as long as the seat next to you is occupied.

Many adults in Britain have a comparable double-take or sense of déjà-vu when they smell carbolic soap. It might happen as they pass through an ironmonger's store. Suddenly it hits them, and they are transported to their childhood years, and to an infant class-room with wash-hand basins, each of which had its own half used block of carbolic soap, guaranteed to spoil the taste of any food which was eaten from hand to mouth in the next four hours.

As with smells, so with songs.

It might not be on the underground, but it might be in the street or in a cafe. It will certainly be unpremeditated. You just happen to be in a place where you hear a song which creates a deep personal reaction – either of love or of loathing as your memory recalls who you were with or what you were doing when that particular song made its greatest impact on you.

I occasionally amuse myself by inviting people to finish the lines of programme or advertising jingles. In Scotland, a favourite is:

Lees, Lees, more if you please.
All of us plead on our bended knees.
For...

and someone will supply the remainder:

...piccaninnies and grandpapas,
it's Lees for luscious macaroon bars.

A more universal ditty, at least in the English-speaking television world, is:

You'll wonder where the yellow went...

to which the appropriate liturgical response is:

...when you brush your teeth with Pepsodent.

On one occasion in North Carolina, where half the audience launched into the second half of the jingle with a mixture of disbelief and laughter, the question was asked as to when and where people had last sung it. The *where* enabled the *when* to be identified, as one woman told of how it reminded her of watching her uncle, whom she regarded as a very handsome man, ironing his shirts in her grandmother's kitchen. From that she was able to ascertain that she had last sung it more than 35 years previously.

And all of us can similarly revisit our past via the songs which root us in that past. I need only hear the first two bars of Jeff Beck's *Heigh Ho, Silver Lining* to be taken back to the joy and risk of running a youth club in the east end of Glasgow where that song was the anthem of a gang called The Crazy Tyne who frequented the club every Saturday night.

For other people, the sound of Bob Dylan's voice singing *You Masters of War* might take them to a 1960s demonstration or smoky folk club. For some, Lennon and McCartney's *Yesterday* will bring to mind a broken romance, while for others any one of ABBA's greatest hits might allow for the revisitation of an embarrassing evening in a karaoke bar. Only time will tell whether in the future the song *Make Me a Channel of Your Peace* will evoke the funeral of Diana, Princess of Wales, as easily as Handel's *Let the Bright Seraphim* evokes her wedding.

We are creatures of our past. We cannot be separated from it, and although we cannot always remember it, songs will unexpectedly summon portions of it into mind. If this is true of secular ballads, it is even more true of Christian songs and hymns, especially those which have been in currency since childhood.

While one person might delight to sing *Be Thou My Vision*, because she likes the Irish tune *Slane* and is making a subjective aesthetic judgement, another person will wince, because it was the 'school hymn' sung every week for six years at Wednesday morning Assembly.

I was once preaching in Northern Ireland, in a Presbyterian church full of people of responsibility and importance in that society. During the course of worship, the congregation were invited to sing *Jesus Loves Me* slowly, seated and unaccompanied.

By the end of the third verse, there was hardly a dry eye in the church, not because it had been an intentionally emotional service, but because the singing of that song took so many people back to their childhood, and to those who nurtured and encouraged them in those important early days.

This bondedness to the past which songs evoke helps explain the unusual nature of some choices of hymn at weddings. When a bride and groom stand before the altar to vow eternal love to each other do they really want to sing

Dear Lord and Father of mankind,
forgive our foolish ways,
reclothe us in our rightful mind...?

Even if, for reasons of penitence before entering into a new covenant, they should wish to sing the first verse, can they really mean all that follows?

Breathe through the heats of our desire
thy coolness and thy balm.
Let sense be dumb, let flesh retire...

But the probability is that the tune, not the words, reminds the bride (or her mother) of some happy occasion. *Repton* is, after all, a beautiful tune. So in the interests of personal reminiscence on the part of a few, the whole congregation is engaged to sing about sinfulness at a celebration of nuptial bliss.

The discerning pastor or pastoral musician has to be able, for the good of the rest of the congregation and the integrity of the event, to help those choosing the hymns to distinguish the difference between what is individually evocative and what is suited for community singing.

More pertinent and sensitive than weddings are funerals. These can be atrociously awkward when the family or friends of the deceased insist on having his favourite tune played, even if it is *I'm Forever Blowing Bubbles.*

A nun in Belfast explained how she coped with this kind of sticky situation. She said that where something would clearly be inappropriate for the requiem mass or crematorium service, she suggested to the family that she would be happy to come to the house or funeral parlour before the public service and, with the family and those for whom it would mean much, play the song or music in the presence of the deceased.

Two other things may be said in this regard.

The first has to do with children's songs. As indicated above, what we learn in childhood we retain all our life and – as discussed in a later chapter – the images of God we receive from such songs will determine our faith and theology. That means that whenever anyone teaches a child a hymn or religious song, they may be preparing that child to meet his or her Maker. Does that seem too extreme?

Then consider the experience of those who minister to the elderly. A hospital chaplain colleague talks of how when she takes prayers in a geriatric ward, where people cannot read hymn texts, she uses the songs they have in their memory. So they will sing *Jesus Loves Me*, and *If I Come to Jesus, He Will Make Me Glad*, both of which not only invoke the past but speak positively of the love of God.

Consider a child born in the 1970s, finding himself coming towards the end of his life in a geriatric ward in the 2060s, and as he prepares to make his peace with God summoning up such a deeply spiritual ditty as:

If I were a fuzzy wuzzy bear,
I'd thank you, Lord,
for my fuzzy wuzzy hair.

Children's hymns should never be seen simply as a form of entertainment to keep the kids happy. These songs, in the future, will be evocative of God.

The other issue relates back to the discussion about what tune best accompanies the text *What a Friend We Have in Jesus*.

When a congregation purchases a new hymn-book, people inevitably flick over the pages not so much to see what new items have been included as to identify which favourite hymns have been 'tampered with' or excluded. And it will often be that the new book is welcomed or damned more by its exclusions than its inclusions.

For many people, the old songs are the best ones. The simple but inarticulated truth is that they have accrued to them a canon of sacred memories and associations. The new items, as yet unknown, have no pedigree of familiarity and fondness.

In 1973, the third edition of *The Church Hymnary* was produced. This hymnal was intended for use primarily in the Presbyterian churches in the four nations constituting the United Kingdom. It was not met with universal acclaim, especially in Northern Ireland where barely a third of the churches invested in the new book.

Much of the dissension gathered around hymns which were omitted, principally two:

What a Friend We Have in Jesus
and
By Cool Siloam's Shady Rill.

For many, the former hymn was evocative of their coming to faith, and they felt insulted, as if their past were insignificant.

For others, their anger was directed at the exclusion of a hymn whose popularity is something of an enigma.

By Cool Siloam's Shady Rill, as it appeared in the previous edition of *The Church Hymnary* was included, in contracted form, in the baptismal section. If all verses had been printed, it could equally well have appeared in the funeral section. Here is the full text:

By cool Siloam's shady rill
how sweet the lily grows!
How sweet the breath beneath the hill
of Sharon's dewy rose.

Lo! such a child whose early feet
the paths of peace have trod,
whose secret heart with influence sweet
is upward drawn to God.

By cool Siloam's shady rill
the lily must decay,
the rose that blooms beneath the hill
must shortly fade away

And soon, too soon, the wintry hour
of man's maturer age
will shake the soul with sorrow's power
and stormy passion's rage.

O thou whose infant feet were found
within thy Father's shrine,

whose years, with changeless virtue crowned,
were all alike divine.

Dependent on thy bounteous breath
we seek thy grace alone,
in childhood, manhood, age and death,
to keep us still thine own.
(Reginald Heber)

Of the four verses which had frequently been sung at baptism (1,2,5 & 6) not one mentions sacrament, water, vows, the promise of God, incorporation into the death of Christ, membership of the community of faith, or the offering of children to be baptised. If there is any childhood theme it is a sentimental allusion to the boyhood of Jesus.

According to those who have visited the Holy Land, the description of the venue in verse one is rather misleading. As one pilgrim suggested, 'The pool of Siloam is just a dirty wee puddle in the Middle East. There were no flowers.'

The tune, *Belmont*, to which the text is set, is not at all inspiring; it seems little more than sequences of descending notes. How, then, did the omission of such a hymn, which was not about baptism, which was geographically inept and which had a half-hearted tune, cause so much offence?

The fact was that for two, if not three, generations of Presbyterians, that hymn and their children's baptisms were inseparable. Excising it from the new hymnal was tantamount to invalidating the efficacy of the baptisms which its singing had accompanied.

As in secular society, so in the Church songs can be highly emotive, because they root us in and remind us of the past, and others will never know how important that past has been for us.

6. To tell stories

Bring the good old bugle, boys,
we'll sing another song,
sing it with a spirit
that will start the world along,
sing it as we used to sing
when fifty thousand strong,
while we were marching through Georgia
(Henry C. Work, USA)

There was a time when every Scottish child was expected to recite from memory substantial poems with opening lines such as:

Half a league, half a league,
half a league onwards

or

The king sits in Dunfermline toun,
drinking his bluid red wine

The first is an historical English epic, the second an important ballad in Scottish literature. Similar kinds of poetry can be found in the written and oral traditions of every nation and culture. They transmit the historical and cultural information from which we gain our identity, know to whom we belong, and sense the bigger picture of which we are a part.

In the days before literacy was commonplace, it was the function of the poets and the storytellers to shape memorable narratives and ballads through which a people learn of the past, thereby helping them to shape the future. Such creative minds were formative in developing a nation or a people's self-understanding.

In some societies, the purveyors of history and tradition did not simply recite texts, but set them to music. In this respect mediaeval minstrels were the forebears of contemporary singer-songwriters who – in the face of computers and e-mail – still believe that the sung record of an event, or the sung tribute to a person's life, is as important as documented history or a comprehensive obituary.

All over the world, this literary transmission of formative stories has been employed. It is not simply the preserve of Welsh bards or Scandinavian saga writers. It is evidenced in the creation myths found in many sub-Saharan tribal cultures. It is found in the great epic poems through which Hindu people tell the story of the activity of their gods, as the ancient Greeks famously did in theirs. It is still gloriously alive in oral cultures such as those of the Australian Aboriginal populations whose capacity to memorise ancient tribal history is only matched by their ability to depict the same in symbolic art. It still surfaces in Scottish folk-clubs where the foibles of government or of the national football team are celebrated in sung verse.

In as many styles as there are cultures, the story of the tribe or nation is told and retold, and those who belong to that tribe or nation feel resonances which do not always transmit to those of another race or culture.

And this very human activity of passing on information through story-poem or song is also found in the Bible. The first chapter of Genesis may be seen as a hymn which celebrates the gradually unfolding creative purposes and potentials of God, each stanza ending with the line:

And there was evening, and there was morning,
the (first) day.

In Exodus chapter 15, we find a song attributed to Moses in which he celebrates what will become known as salvation history.

The enemy boasted, 'I shall pursue, I shall overtake;
I shall divide the spoil,
I shall glut my appetite on them;
I shall draw my sword,
I shall rid myself of them. '
You blew with your blast; the sea covered them;
they sank like lead in the swelling waves.
(Exodus 15:9–10)

This same reinvoking of the deliverance of the people, sometimes accompanied by a rehearsal of their sins and waywardness, can be found in several of the Psalms, notably Psalms 105 and 106:

Then Israel too went down into Egypt
Jacob came to live in the land of Ham.
There God made his people very fruitful,
too numerous for their enemies,
whose hearts he turned to the hatred of his people,
to double-dealing with his servants.
He sent his servant Moses
and Aaron whom he had chosen.
(Psalm 105:23–26)

Disbelieving God's promise,
they rejected the pleasant land.
They muttered treason in their tents,
and would not obey the Lord.
So with hand uplifted he made an oath
to strike them down in the wilderness.
(Psalm 106:24–26)

Even in the New Testament, which covers a relatively short compass of human experience compared with the Old, there is evidence of songs written to let a story be told. Chapter two of the Letter to the Philippians has one such example. It celebrates the culmination of salvation history – the death and resurrection of Jesus.

Here it is, first in prose and then in a metrical setting which can be sung to the tune *Jerusalem*.

He was in the form of God; yet he laid no claim to equality with God, but made himself nothing, assuming the form of a slave. Bearing the human likeness, sharing the human lot, he humbled himself, and was obedient even to the point of death, death on a cross! Therefore God raised him to the heights and bestowed on him the name above all names, that at the name of Jesus every knee should bow – in heaven, on earth, and in the depths – and every tongue acclaim, 'Jesus is Lord,' to the glory of God the Father.
(Philippians 2:6–11)

Though one with God, yet not by might
did Christ his equal status claim:
instead he gave up all he had
and as a humble servant came.
In worldly form, of woman born,
he lived at one with humankind
and strode and stumbled to the cross
that we the path to life might find.

Therefore God raised him after death,
raised him to reign in earth and heaven:
the one whom we considered least,
the greatest name by God was given.
And so, to honour Jesus' name,

all who have life or are to be
shall kneel proclaiming, 'Christ is Lord!'
and worship God eternally.

What all these examples have in common is objectivity. They are not subjective accounts of personal experience, nor are they primarily theological musings on important events. They simply tell what happened in order that future generations might learn the facts and appropriate the significance for themselves.

This puts down a marker about the kind of songs which we select to sing in church. For if personal choice of the leaders, or congregational favourites, or those with the brightest tunes are the main considerations, we may end up bathing in sentimentality and subjectivism.

As long as the Gospel is regarded as public truth, there have to be songs which tell – albeit in contemporary language – the old, old story of God's dealings with humanity, especially in Christ.

7. To shape the future

Somewhere over the rainbow,
way up high,
there's a land that I heard of
once in a lullaby.

Occasionally English people wonder why there is such a wealth of folk songs from Ireland, Scotland and Wales, yet relatively few from England, despite its having the largest population of the four nations.

There are a number of plausible reasons.

One is that England, having the capital city and the court, was more liable to be affected by and encourage 'serious music' than those parts of Great Britain geographically furthest from London. A capital city naturally attracts to itself visitors, performers and impresarios from abroad and, especially in previous eras, would be a seed bed for musical creativity which would eventually affect the regions closest to it.

Another reason for the paucity of English folksong has to do with the effect of industrialisation in the 18th and 19th centuries.

People were forced or encouraged to leave rural areas and live in growing conurbations such as Birmingham, Manchester and Leeds. The resulting loss of extended families in rural areas contributed also to a loss in folk culture which these families had hitherto kept alive.

It was indeed a great blessing that musicians such as Vaughan Williams and Cecil Sharpe, perceiving the slow death of rural folk music, did so much at the beginning of the 20th century to transcribe what was still in the memory of older country people.

But there is a third reason, a little less obvious, which is associated with the other two. It is that during the imperial era, when Britain was fighting battles and colonising the globe, there were deliberate moves by the government of the day to foster popular support for overseas 'projects' by encouraging the singing of attractive songs and ditties whose implicit message was one of positive affirmation of Britain's exploits.

Writers and composers were encouraged to produce words and music for what became known as 'national songs'. They included such defiant odes as:

Rule, Britannia
The British Grenadiers
Hearts of Oak

They appeared, until recently, in collections often including some of the more popular English folk songs like *Greensleeves* and *O Waly Waly*, and some other parlour ditties such as *Little Brown Jug* and *There's No Place Like Home.*

Although precise evidence would be hard to assemble, there is good reason to suspect that the politically encouraged songs gradually eroded interest in the indigenous folk material which in an urban setting would not resonate as it had in rural areas.

Conversations with a French musicologist suggested that exactly the same thing happened in France from the Napoleonic period onwards. National songs – of which *La Marseillaise* is the best known – were promulgated in the large centres of population. It is now mainly in the rural and coastal areas such as Brittany and Normandy that the indigenous folk literature is still alive.

This may come as a surprise to people who thought that it was only Germany, in the days of the Goebbels culture ministry, or Stalinist Russia with its oppression of free-thinking composers like Shostakovitch which manipulated song and music to increase popular support for political causes.

Attending a performance of Joan Littlewood's *Oh What a Lovely War* provides a necessary corrective. For this musical, set amidst the horror of the First World War trenches, uses the songs of that era which were intended to steel the nerves for the fight and to deal euphemistically with tragedy and gruelling circumstances.

More immediately accessible to most people may be the lyrics sung by Vera Lynn for comfort and encouragement during World War II:

Oh there's no place like home for a holiday

There'll be blue birds over the white cliffs of Dover

Such songs were not innocent ditties with catchy tunes written mainly for pleasure. Their purposes were political. They were part of government propaganda to get the nation behind the war effort.

Now, what has all this to do with the purpose of this chapter, let alone this book? And what has it to do with the music of the Church?

It is simply to illustrate from a secular context what is equally true in a religious one, namely that what we sing informs and indeed shapes what we believe. Singing is not a neutral exercise. It should carry a government health warning that it can affect minds.

That is one of the principal reasons for singing in the Church. In our song we do not simply versify what is written in the Bible. We also state what we hold to be true about life and God, in the hope that those who sing the verses will believe them.

It is salutory in this respect to describe what the Iona Community's Wild Goose Resource Group has consistently found over 15 years of working in the area of public worship and liturgy.

When the group asks people to recount what for them has been a significant worship experience, only one in a hundred ever mention a sermon – and those who do are usually preachers. More commonly people will talk about a song, a silence, a symbolic action, a service of worship in an unusual place. And yet clergy commonly hold that it is the sermon or homily which primarily informs people's thinking about God. This is arrogant presumption. It is much more what they sing that shapes their faith. For when the most memorable line of the most rhetorically astute sermon has been forgotten, people will remember the words of *Abide With Me*, or *Love Divine, All Loves Excelling*, or *Majesty*.

And they will remember such texts because, unlike sermons, the same combination of words will be used on many occasions. And, unlike sermons, the words will be in verse, set to a tune, both of which aid memory.

And people will remember them because of the truth in the basic educational maxim:

WHAT I HEAR, I FORGET,
WHAT I SEE, I REMEMBER,
WHAT I DO, I UNDERSTAND.

Singing is a hearing and seeing and, above all, doing activity. It requires us to take into ourselves and circulate through our system words and music which others have written and, for a shorter or longer period, to make these our own.

What the Church sings, therefore, is determinative of the faith which the singers hold.

At this juncture, it is tempting to give a thousand testimonies from different people about how what they sang – especially in childhood – has affected their faith for good or ill.

In the interests of brevity, we will attend to three aspects of faith which are open to the influence of the songs we sing: theology, Christology and missiology…or what we believe about God, Jesus, and the mission of the Church.

THEOLOGY

A number of years ago, I was invited to be a visiting professor at Bangor Seminary, Maine. One of the responsibilities was to teach a course in church music.

Students were asked in advance to submit essays on how the songs of their childhood had affected their understanding of God. All the submissions were salutory.

One woman had been brought up in the Roman Catholic Church prior to Vatican II. Although the songs she had sung as a child were unintelligible through being in Latin, from these songs she had inherited a sense that God was 'warm and mysterious, not frightening, just wonderful'. She had sung songs like

O magnum mysterium
and
Tantum ergo sacramentum

A Protestant man had grown up in a strict Calvinist environment. He had sensed from his childhood hymns that God was eternally angry, judgemental, and curious about the minutiae of everyone's failings. He also had an underdeveloped notion of the importance of Jesus, since the adult church tended to sing psalms which do not explicitly mention the Saviour's name.

Among the children's hymns he sang were:

Do no sinful action, speak no angry word
and

God is always near me, hearing what I say.

Then there was a man who had grown up in a redemptionist background where hymns with military imagery were very popular. He had sung texts such as:

Onward, Christian Soldiers,
Dare to Be a Daniel
When the Roll is Called Up Yonder
Soldiers of Christ, Arise

During the Vietnam war, this man was conscripted. He went in as a believer and came out as an atheist. Part of the reason was that in the army there were reprises in military church services of the songs he had sung since childhood. But he could not believe that the butchery he was involved in could be at all consonant with a reputedly loving God. He did not want to know that God.

Only later in life was he able to distance himself from the icon of a predominantly militaristic deity, and meet – as for the first time – the God and Father of our Lord Jesus Christ.

What we sing shapes the way we understand and think of God.

CHRISTOLOGY

It also affects the way we think about, understand and follow Jesus.

I was once asked by an Australian pastor to lead a men's Bible study in a church in a remote part of New South Wales.

Around twelve men appeared for this early on a Wednesday morning. The passage chosen for discussion was the miracle of the raising of Lazarus in John's Gospel.

The passage was read over in the New English Bible translation so that all might hear and it was suggested that if any words seemed unclear, these should be dealt with before the passage was explored in depth.

One of the group, a medical consultant, asked what the word 'indignation' meant, as it was used to describe Jesus' reaction to the grief shown by Mary, Lazarus's sister:

When Jesus saw her weeping and the Jews who had come with her weeping, he was moved with indignation and deeply distressed. (John 11:33)

When it was pointed out that the word meant angry, the doctor became visibly distressed himself.

'That can't possibly be true,' he protested. 'I have followed Jesus Christ all my life and I have never known him to be angry!'

Behind that protestation there may have been a man who could not deal with his own anger and therefore did not want to think of Jesus having to cope with a similar human dilemma. Or, more probably, there was a man who had been reared on a hymnal published in 1927 for use in the Presbyterian churches of Great Britain, and New Zealand, Australia and South Africa. In this book one not only finds children's hymns such as:

Gentle Jesus, Meek and Mild

but also lines in adult hymns such as:

No one marked an angry word
who ever heard him speak.

By and large, our songs about Jesus are deficient. They deal, in the main, with his birth or death. They seldom deal with recurrent themes of his life such as the inclusion of outsiders, the enjoyment of food, anger at injustice and an acceptance and appreciation of women.

And what they say regarding the birth or early life of Jesus is often far from the truth.

Take, for example, the carol *Away in a Manger*. The first verse might be adequate, but ponder this:

The cattle are lowing, the baby awakes,
but little Lord Jesus no crying he makes.

Why not? Every other human baby does. What a contrast with the more apt description of the seventeenth-century hymnwriter Thomas Pestel:

Hark, hark, the wise eternal Word
like a weak infant cries.

And as we progress into the childhood of Jesus, can we really claim that:

And through all his wondrous childhood,
he would honour and obey,

watch and love the lowly maiden
in whose gentle arms he lay?
(From *Once in Royal David's City* by Cecil Francis Alexander)

...especially when the 'wondrous childhood' would go right up to his Barmitzvah, and especially when the only thing we know about that era in Jesus' life is that he ran away from his parents when he was twelve.

Perhaps it is all a ploy to make Jesus out to be the most docile of creatures in order that:

Christian children all must be
mild, obedient, good as he.

It is not the divinity of Christ that our hymns need to extol. We have plenty of texts which are sung to Jesus on the throne. It is the glorious incarnation, which puts a new value on human life and reveals the true nature of God, that calls out to be celebrated in word and song in order that our discipleship might be informed by the true example of Jesus.

MISSIOLOGY

Then there is missiology, or what we believe about the mission of the Church.

In the late 1980s the Wild Goose Worship Group was asked to sing at a missionary rally in Glasgow. It attracted almost 700 people per year; and it enabled the Church of Scotland to inform people about its work overseas and to let them hear the testimonies of those who had been working abroad.

Because South Africa and the Philippines were going to be featured, and because the Group had recently learned songs from these countries, it was decided that these would be taught to the gathering in the twenty minutes of musical 'warm-up' prior to the rally proper.

There was a marked reluctance in the hall to entertain such songs. People were visibly and audibly resistant. This seemed unusual because the same songs had received an enthusiastic response when sung in the open air at anti-apartheid meetings. However, when the time came for the old missionary hymns, these were sung treble forte and gutsioso.

The assembly roared to God about how

Oe'r heathen lands afar
thick darkness broodeth yet

…despite the fact that in parts of Asia and Africa church growth was in inverse proportion to church decline in the UK, and despite the fact that there were Christian settlements in North Africa and India centuries before there was significant missionary activity in Scotland.

The reason for the reluctance to sing the songs of churches abroad was a result of years of subliminal persuasion, via the texts of hymns, that the rest of the world was what we gave to, not what we took from. Any notion of solidarity in the body of Christ, of reciprocation of ministry, of mutual encouragement, was alien to the missionary preconceptions of those who had been brought up to sing about the plight of God's 'sun-kissed' children, not to share their potential. For many, the seeds of this religious imperialism were planted in childhood.

There was a children's song sung in Sunday Schools until the 1970s which went:

Do you see this penny?
It is brought by me
for the little children
far across the sea.
Hurry, penny, quickly
though you are so small;
help to tell the heathen
Jesus loves them all.
(Featured in collections of children's songs by Carey Bonar)

In some Sunday Schools, while this was being sung, children would trot out to the front of the class where the miniature metal torso of a black man sat on a table. It had two rows of white teeth opened wide, and an arm attached, the hand of which rested just below the chin. Children put a penny on the palm of the hand, twisted 'Sambo's' ear and he swallowed the penny.

Imagine what that inculcated in the young about Britain's relationship to the developing world!

This may seem like a catalogue of woes about the damage which inaccurate words can do as they affect the faith of those who sing and believe them. So let a more positive story vindicate the claim that what we sing can work for good.

In 1993, I visited St Louis, USA, and at a Pastoral Musician's Convention introduced church musicians to musical literature from the Global Church. Four years later, I was in the neighbouring Roman Catholic diocese of Bellville, where a number of people talked about the effect which songs from around the world had had on children to whom they had been taught.

Not only did the children (unlike so many adults) jump at the opportunity of singing the songs both in English and the indigenous language, but parents were reporting that when there was a news headline about Zimbabwe their sons or daughters would burst into *Jesu, Tawa Pano*. Or if Argentina were mentioned, they might begin to sing *Santo, Santo, Santo*.

The people who told these stories were all involved in Christian education, either in school or church, and they claimed that children exposed to this multicultural kind of music had a far more integrated idea of the world than they (the teachers) had had as children. And they were proud that it was the Church which was enabling this most positive development.

If space permitted, we could look at how our hymns and songs enable or inhibit our understanding of evangelism, discipleship, public witness and a host of other things, For the moment let it be sufficient to admit that what we sing shapes what we believe.

8. To enable work

Hullamackadoo hoorovahee
Hoorova hinda hoorova hinda
(Gaelic Spinning Song)

There were two musical phenomena in Britain in the 1950s and 60s which popularised negro spirituals.

The first, mentioned earlier, was a Saturday night television show which was a non-stop performance of choreographed songs, sung by around 18 white men whose faces had been painted black and who were accompanied by an equal number of white women who retained their natural skin colouring.

The *Black and White Minstrel Show* was a very successful programme, compulsory viewing for many people who liked 'family entertainment'. Among ballads by such well known 'black' composers as Noel Coward and Jerome Kern were interspersed songs by Stephen Foster and the occasional spiritual, sometimes sung at breakneck speed accompanied by a banjo.

An entirely different phenomenon was the Glasgow Orpheus Choir, conducted by a local undertaker called Sir Hugh Roberton.

They also, in concert dress, sang negro spirituals, but they rarely sang them at stirring tempi or with a faked Afro-American accent.

Roberton's arrangements might sound a little precious to modern ears, but in its time the sound of the Orpheus Choir was emulated all over Scotland, as spirituals such as *Steal Away to Jesus* were sung with breathy rubato and an almost crematorium-like solemnity.

What neither the Black and White Minstrels nor the Orpheus Choir did was to pay respect to the origins of their favoured songs.

For negro spirituals are not first and foremost either entertainment songs or masterpieces for choral recital. They were originally work songs. And as well as being religious they could also be subversive, for underneath the piety of such texts as *The Gospel Train's a Comin'* or even *Steal Away to Jesus* there might be an encoded message about the availability of a means of escape to take slaves across not the Jordan but the Ohio river and onto Harriet Tubman's underground railway which would deliver them to freedom further north in America.

The work which these songs accompanied was often backbreaking and dangerous. Cutting sugar cane, laying track, chipping stones required a regular and common rhythm in the work force. This was especially true for gangs of men chained to each other using pickaxes. To ensure the safety of all, the picks had to be raised and lowered at the same time, and one way of achieving this was either to have all the men singing together or to have the song led by one individual on a call and response basis.

There is a marvellous recording made by the Afro-American

singer Pamella Warrick Smith, entitled *Work, Fight and Pray*. With a vocal range extending from the C below what most men can sing to the C above what most women aspire to, she sings chain-gang and other work songs with a chorus responding as would have happened in the original setting.

These songs, some of which were collected on the Georgia Sea Islands, bear a close resemblance to the styles of corporate song found in Western Africa (from which many of the original slaves came). There, as elsewhere in Africa, songs have been the means which enabled work to get done, whether that work was tilling the land, moving into battle, preparing a feast or nursing children.

But it is not just those of African heritage who sing songs originally used for enabling work. Similar examples can be found in the folk heritage of any nation. What now pass for jovial community songs in folk clubs would originally have accompanied and enabled the working processes of daily life.

In Scotland *The Mingulay Boat Song* originally helped men to pull together on the oars, especially when rowing against a running tide. *The Lewis Bridal Song* enabled people in a bridal procession to move from place to place without their spirits flagging. *Dream Angus* was used by women to encourage sleep in wide-awake children. And there are songs for spinning, for weaving, even for wauking (or stretching) tweed cloth. And what are sea shanties originally but the songs by which men pulled up anchors, spread sails or climbed masts?

Songs, because of the regularity of their rhythm, enable

work to get done.

We have seen this to good effect in the kitchen of Iona Abbey where up to twelve people may be washing and drying dishes after a meal for seventy in the Refectory. Whether it is South African freedom songs in four-part harmony, or standards from the shows, the act of singing together gets the work done quickly and cheerfully.

And this is true for the worship of the Church also.

The term 'liturgy' is derived from two Greek words which mean the work of the people. Like many religious terms such as redemption and salvation, its origins are in the secular world. For the liturgy to happen, songs are needed both to incorporate the whole community, thus saving worship from being a priestly function only, and to enable the various aspects of the service to flow.

We need songs which will allude to or illuminate the reason for our gathering, prioritise the reading of scripture, and affirm the commitment of God's people to the purposes of their Maker. We need songs which enable the Church on earth to be bonded to the Church in heaven – thus we sing the *Sanctus*, the 'Holy, Holy' which Isaiah heard and which John the Divine witnessed.

We need an *Amen* to allow the congregation to give its assent to the prayers or blessing offered by the officiant, and – depending on our tradition – we might need songs which encourage and enable worshippers to come forward and receive the eucharist.

Both from ancient traditions in Britain and from the experience of churches in countries where people may congregate in an open space to worship we discover gathering songs which summon people together and let them know the reason for their meeting. If there is a processional or recessional in which the leaders of worship or sectors of the congregation have to move in public, an appropriate text sung to an engaging tune – such as *Come, All You People* from Zimbabwe, will enable that movement to happen.

It is thus insufficient merely to have hymns which rehearse theology or articulate what we feel. For worship to move, there have to be words and music which undergird and encourage emotional, psychological and physical activity.

Singing in church is not the religious equivalent of television commercials to offer relief between prolonged periods of speech. Singing in church is a means by which the worship of those committed to Christ is enabled to happen with engagement and integrity.

9. To exercise our creativity

Ama - (AMA) - zing love
How can - (HOW CAN) - it be
That thou, - (THAT THOU) - my God,
shouldst die for me.
Charles Wesley (to the tune *Sagina*)

Creativity is an odd concept.

We believe that painters and sculptors are creative, because they manufacture works of art. We extend the category to include potters, engravers, wood workers and glass blowers – again they provide visible evidence of their talent.

We also call authors, poets and playwrights creative, because what they invent ends up in print or on stage; and we use the term to cover instrumentalists, singers, actors and dancers, believing that their skills in interpreting music, text or movement are part of the 'creative' process.

We are not so sure about landscape gardeners, town planners or interior decorators; even less sure about preachers, civil engineers and cooks; and question whether the term could ever possibly be associated with bakers and florists.

It is astounding sometimes to go for a meal in a house where the mother of five children has not only prepared a sumptuous feast, but has herself made the tablecloth and napkins, bottled the jam and chutney, arranged the display of roses and carnations at the centre of the dining table, chosen and perfectly matched the decor and furniture, and may even have painted and papered the room in question. Yet she would not claim to be 'a very creative person'.

All who are made in the image of God are creative, because God whose image we bear is first revealed in scripture as the great Creator. And when we sing we engage in a creative process. For the moment we open our mouths to sing we are putting our own interpretation on what the words and music mean.

It is interesting, in this respect, to listen to two different people – performers or lounge bar crooners – singing the same song, the latter especially if they have had a few.

Take an old country and western standard such as:

Put your sweet lips a little closer to the phone,
let's pretend that we're together, all alone.
I'll tell the man to turn the juke-box way down low,
and you can tell your friend there with you
he'll have to go.
(A. Allison/J. Allison)

One person will emphasise the word *sweet*, another the word *lips*. One will quieten her voice at the end of line three and sing the last two lines with pathos. Another will get louder at the same place and make the last two lines sound like an undefiable command. Drunk or sober, the singer is engaging his or her creativity in the performance of the song.

In Scotland, when there is a ceilidh among friends, certain people will be asked to sing particular songs, not because they are the only folk who can remember the words, but because somehow the inflection in their voice, even if it is half-rusty, brings the text to life.

Of all the arts music opens itself to the greatest degree of participation and creativity. A painting can be seen by everyone. It is a passive experience, not a physically demanding one. A play can be read or performed by actors, but not everyone will speak at the same time, and for its best performance it needs good rehearsal and an attentive audience.

Poetry can be an intensely private thing, requiring the words to be repeated over and over again until all the nuances and allusions are recognised. And even if read aloud by the author, there is no guarantee that the poem will instantly communicate its meaning.

Dance – especially ballet or ballroom – requires skill and nimbleness. For its best exposition, trained performers are required.

But when we come to music, and especially to community singing, there is no particular requirement of expertise, nor is there the need for a passive audience. All can participate.

Even more curiously, music, unlike art or literature, does not live when it is inscribed on a piece of paper. Only a very few people are able to pick up an orchestral or choral score and instantly hear how it will sound when played or sung. The notes mean nothing nor do they look aesthetically pleasing when they are on the page. The song comes alive when people use their breath to articulate the intended sounds. It has to be an external thing.

Thirty people could read the same one-act play and use their imagination to visualise it and their intellect to understand it. It might be a very pleasurable exercise. But the same could not happen with thirty people reading the same song.

Only when voices physically engage in its performance does the notation become an experience. Then creativity is at work in every singer, even if we do not always name it.

10. To give of ourselves

...I, being poor, have only my dreams.

I have spread my dreams under your feet;
Tread softly, because you tread on my dreams

W.B. Yeats

When I was a teenager, I spent two summers working as a van-boy for a local hauliers. I was put to work with a man called Tam who had a lovely wife called Rita, and two young sons.

Tam had a beautiful tenor voice, and he had no embarrassment about bursting into song as he drove, dug the garden or played with his children.

It was Rita who revealed that his voice was one of the main reasons why she had married him. In their courting days, they would go for long walks in the Ayrshire countryside and sometimes when they stopped for a rest, Tam would face Rita and with abject sincerity and delight sing:

Oh my love is like a red, red rose,
that's newly sprung in June;

Oh my love is like a violin
that's sweetly played in tune.
As fair art thou, my bonnie lass,
sae deep in love am I,
and I will love you still, my dear,
till a' the seas gang dry.

Inevitably, Rita would be reduced to tears and helplessness in the face of this deeply moving rendition of a song by Robert Burns.

It wasn't simply what he sang, it was the fact *that* he sang and sang this song only for her.

When we sing we do something unique. For – never mind the song – there is no voice which sounds like ours. It is part of our imaging in the likeness of God. As God is unique, so are we; as God's voice is singular, so is each of ours.

As indicated previously, when we speak alone or together, there is nothing peculiarly startling about it. But when we sing, and enliven the text through music, and enter into that music not just with our mouth and ears, but with our whole being, then we are doing something which is both personal and holistic.

And if this utterance of song is offered to someone else, then we may be sure that it is a unique gift which no one else could offer. For no one else has our voice, and the song will last only for as long as we sing it. Then it is gone, and no one else will hear that particular rendering.

One of the reasons why people go to concerts to hear anyone from Pavarotti to Shirley Bassey is because they believe that when these peculiar voices engage with their selected songs, it will be an unrepeatable event. It will not be like a taped recording, because most recordings are done in a studio with plenty of technical gadgetry to intimidate but no live audience to inspire.

When an artiste is confronted with a particular audience in a particular hall on a particular evening, there is a magic in the air as he or she may give a completely new inflection to a song which they might have sung hundreds of times before.

And reviewers of concerts really get excited when they are present at a performance of a work they have heard many times, but on this occasion the soloist or the choir or the orchestra offers something extra which creates a frisson of awareness and connectedness in the audience. On such an occasion, the audience feels moved and blessed.

One of the purposes of singing in church, especially by a choir or a soloist, is to enable that transforming experience to happen.

In this respect, singing can be truly evangelical. The late Leon Roberts was an Afro-American composer and church musician who came from Baptist roots but converted to Catholicism and worked in the parish of St Augustine's in Washington DC. As a result of a moment of deep personal intimacy with God, he wrote a setting of the Magnificat, entitled *Mary's Song*. This involves a female soloist singing the text of the Magnificat in association with a choir which repeats a fairly simple antiphon:

My being declares the goodness of the Lord;
my spirit is glad in God my Saviour.

I have heard this sung by a concert soloist who enunciated every note perfectly and gave a flawless performance. But the time when it really came alive was when Leon was doing a workshop in Cincinnati, demonstrating to a mostly white audience how black people sing.

He asked if anyone knew his setting well enough to sing it. In the front row, a number of black women pointed to the same friend, a woman in her fifties who agreed to take the solo in this workshop situation.

The woman was sturdy and had a face which told a lot of stories. She was no shrinking madonna. As the song evolved, her soul caught fire, and she sang that defiant manifesto of the revolutionary nature of God's kingdom with passion and conviction, the sweat flying from her brow as she enunciated ever more defiantly:

He has filled the hungry with good things,
but the rich he has sent empty away.

For the duration of that song, she was Mary and we in the workshop were present at the annunciation, and all were strangely moved.

However, it is not simply to move, to convert, to influence others that we sing in church. The object or recipient of our singing is not those standing around us, but God, to whom our worship is offered.

And so something extremely rare happens whenever a congregation sings to its Maker. For not only are there ten or fifty or five hundred individual voices giving their unique gift as they open their mouths and sing; there is also the unique blending of high and low voices, sharp and flat, sophisticated and rough-tongued, male and female, old and young.

The chances are that never again will every one of these people be in exactly the same place singing these particular hymns and songs. At the next service of worship some will be missing, others will be new and the likelihood is that the liturgy will require a different selection of texts for singing.

So, if we can but sense it, every time a congregation sings, it is offering an absolutely one-time-only gift to its Maker. It is important that every song sung is offered to God with that sense of uniqueness. God is worth it.

11. To obey a command

Number eleven was intentionally omitted from the contents list. Read on...

Do-be-do-be-do-be-do-be-do!
(Anon)

It is commonly believed that God gave Moses ten commandments.

The possibility is that God gave eleven, but that Moses didn't have enough room on the stone tablets to engrave the final one, so God had to wait until David came along and let the forgotten decree be heard: 'Sing a new song!'

That this is a divine command and not a human option can be gleaned from the fact that the words *Sing a new song!* do not appear just once in the Bible, but are explicitly stated in Psalms 33, 40, 96, 98, 144 and 149.

Echoes or intimations of God's expectation can also be found in Exodus, Numbers, Judges, Chronicles, Isaiah, Jeremiah, Zephaniah, Zechariah, Matthew, Acts, Philippians, James and Revelation.

While all the previous reasons for singing may be healthily

affirmed in the secular as well as the sacred sphere, singing a new song in obedience to the divine command and expectation is something which is only pertinent to people of faith.

As to why God wanted new songs, we can only conjecture. It may be that God was fed up with the old ones – despite the people's affection for their favourites, which they presumed to be God's favourites too.

We see this in the prophecy of Amos where God astonishes the participants in a primitive praise band by saying,

Stop your noisy songs!
I do not want to listen to the sound of your harps.
(for which read guitars and/or organs)

What lay behind this outburst was the fact that for the community of faith, harmless hymns had become a substitute for action on matters of social justice. And God would not let that be. God wanted not simply praise from the head or heart, but commitment of body, mind and spirit.

This is one good reason for ensuring that people in charge of the music for worship see themselves as part of a greater picture of congregational life and witness, not some autonomous sector dedicated to providing beautiful sounds as a relief from what might be turgid preaching or dull congregational life.

When the song of the church has become tantamount to sentimentality or deliberately avoids the hard issues of the day or the real issues in people's lives, God has every right to tell us to shut up.

But from a more human perspective, and allied to our discovery that songs are part of our gift to God, there are perhaps two reasons why we need to sing new songs.

1. NEW SKINS FOR NEW WINE

The first is captured in the Latin nostrum:

Tempora mutantur
et nos mutamur in illis

(Times change,
and we change in them)

Today is not the same as yesterday, and what was good reason for praise or complaint in the past may not hold true in the future. This is perfectly biblical.

We do not know what the Hebrews sang when they were in captivity in Egypt. It may well have been a primitive protest song which resembled

Go down, Moses,
way down in Egypt's land.
Tell ole Pharaoh
to let my people go.

But whatever it was, that song would be forgotten once people had arrived on the other side of the Red Sea. After such a decisive deliverance, a new song was needed:

Sing to the Lord,
for he has risen up in triumph;
horse and rider
he has hurled into the sea (Exodus 15:21)

...so sang Miriam, a progenitor of General Booth, with her tambourine in hand.

Later, when God's chosen people, or vineyard, had grown deaf or immune to the will of their Maker, another new song was needed to startle them into the reality of God's displeasure. Isaiah penned it:

My beloved had a vineyard
high up on a fertile slope.
He trenched it and cleared it of stones
and planted it with choice vines...

Now listen while I tell you
what I am about to do to my vineyard;
I shall take away its hedge
and let it go to waste.   (Isaiah 5:2&7)

New songs are required and appear all through the Bible. This reality continues right into heaven where, according to the book of Revelation, as well as singing the old song of Moses (Rev. 15:3ff) and the song heard by Isaiah (Rev. 4:8), the inhabitants join in a new song:

You are worthy to receive the scroll
and break its seals,
for you were slain
and by your blood you bought for God
people of every tribe and language, nation and race.
You have made them a royal house of priests for our God,
and they shall reign on earth. (Rev. 5:9)

The Church has always encouraged, resisted evoked, revoked, argued about and eventually accepted new songs.

Although it is hard to believe, the text *I Heard the Voice of Jesus* was once a revolutionary new song. It was needed – at least in the mind of Horatius Bonar, the author – because there was a lack of devotional material to express personal commitment in the present tense. The congregation of which Bonar was minister was not so impressed and forbade it and the rest of his ditties from being sung in public worship.

Sometimes it may be the inadequacy of the existing repertoire but sometimes it is concrete social and political realities which inspire or require new songs.

In the mid-19th century there was a spate of hymnwriting about heaven which depicted children dressed in white nightgowns wandering around the Elysian fields hand in hand with Jesus.

Some of these hymns, such as *If I Come to Jesus*, have made their way into the mainstream of adult piety. But they were not first intended to satisfy an adult demand for hymns of personal devotion. They were written, often in industrial England, in direct response to the scandalously high child mortality rate caused – especially in the great cities – by inadequate pre and post natal care, insanitary living conditions, malnutrition and rickets, and the excesses of child labour in the mines and factories.

Someone had to respond to the remaining siblings who asked of their deceased brothers and sisters, 'Where has Larry gone?' 'Where is Jennifer now?'

New songs were needed, because the old songs did not deal with the current harsh realities of life.

Around the same time in the USA there were a number of poets and hymnwriters whose conscience about slavery and the need to dissociate the Christian Church from that barbarous and inhuman practice impelled them to write new songs such as this by James Russel Lowell:

Men whose boast it is that ye
come of fathers brave and free;
if there breathe on earth a slave
are ye truly free and brave?
If ye do not feel the chain
when it works a brother's pain,
are ye not base slaves indeed,
slaves unworthy to be freed?

The sad reality is that these songs, so revolutionary in their day, have passed into the realms of safe, sacred standards, and the existence of so many 'good old hymns' has been cited as a reason to resist or discourage any new ones.

But the fact is that God wills all things to change and this divine impulse is seen at work in the new realities which bless or beleaguer us.

At the beginning of the 21st century, issues of global pollution, environmental abuse, ethnic cleansing, the development of self-awareness and self-confidence in women and people of colour, the integration of global economies, increasing ecumenical cooperation and a thousand other realities are every bit as deserving of being articulated in a new song as the issues of child mortality and slavery were in the past. But will the Church allow them to find a place in worship?

It is not a matter of aesthetic or liturgical taste. It is a matter of obedience to a divine command and of admitting that the old skins cannot hold new wine.

2. AN INDEX OF LOVE

But there is another reason why it is important to sing new songs.

Every weekday in Iona Abbey, morning prayer ends with words such as these:

This is the day that the Lord has made:
WE WILL REJOICE AND BE GLAD IN IT.
We will not offer to the Lord
OFFERINGS THAT COST US NOTHING.
Go in peace and serve the Lord;
WE WILL SEEK PEACE AND PURSUE IT.

The second sentence is particularly interesting. The words come from the last chapter of the second book of Samuel in which David is determined to make a fitting sacrifice to the Lord.

The words allow worshippers to indicate the value that God has in their lives, and they challenge us to question whether what we give to God are worthless offerings, half-hearted gifts, cheap or cheapened praise.

The worship of God is not a casual thing. It is an expression of worth. That is what worship, or *worth-ship*, means. Worship which is offered with little forethought or preparation, worship which is shoddy and badly led, is not simply an inconvenience to the congregation, it is an insult to the Almighty.

If we imagine, for a moment, deciding to give a present to a friend, we might realise that the care we take in choosing that present is an indication of his or her value in our lives. The first bunch of flowers in the florist's shop, the first bland tie in the box, the first box of chocolates on the shelf may be convenient, but will not necessarily please our friend. That which is chosen with time and imagination, that which costs more than money, will be the valued gift.

A friend recently spoke of his fiftieth birthday party. Paul has many interests, several of which lie in the arts world, for he is an actor, sculptor and inventor. He likes the way in which things piece together and separate.

He is a slightly difficult person for whom to choose a present as he has no evident needs and leads a relatively simple and contented life.

It was therefore a great joy for him to discover that for his birthday two of his friends had cooperated with each other. One who had some money and a lively imagination commissioned one of Paul's fellow sculptors to make nine beautiful pottery animals. On their own, each looks exquisite; side by side they are a delight. But, even more ingenious, they are so made that the animals can stand on top of each other to make a pyramid, with a dog at the summit supporting a hare on its back.

Paul was thrilled...by the craftsmanship, by the novelty and also by the imagination of his two friends who had made sure that he had a gift which had willingly cost them time, money, imagination and physical effort.

And is God worth less?

Is God worth simply the routine songs played by an organist or praise band who believe that they only need to practise solo pieces, not the accompaniment to the hymns?

Is God only worth the rather tired repertoire of the choir which trots out the same old favourites whether or not they accord with the season or there are sufficient voices to do justice to the anthem?

Is God only worth the congregation's favourite hymns, as if the object of worship were to titillate the ears of the singers and not offer real and deep praise to their Maker?

Any relationship which is going anywhere involves people discovering more about each other, and behaving in ways which express that understanding.

If a man were to discover five years after marriage that the

Chanel he always brought back for his wife after a trip abroad actually brought on her allergies, he would, in the light of that information, change the gift he gave her. Or if a woman were to discover that, despite her own literary predilections, her companion liked nothing better than to read a blood-chilling murder story, then that information should inform her choice of book when buying one for her friend's birthday.

Every day is the birthday of God, and every day God is deserving of words and music which celebrate God's magnificence, generosity and imagination. Therefore, not for a moment disregarding that which has proven its value in worship, we must yet sing God new songs as a sign that our love of God is lively and not tired, expectant and not presumptuous.

SECTION TWO

Why do people not sing?

IF, dear reader, you have turned to this section before reading the previous one, then go no further. In Church music we have to live out of the positives rather than the negatives, to celebrate what all can do rather than gloat on what some cannot manage.

BUT if you have fulfilled all righteousness by reading this book in chronological order, then be aware that the following pages may be a little disquieting. This will be especially so if you are a music teacher, church organist, church architect or the leading alto who thought she should have made Covent Garden but nobody agreed with her. And even more so if you are someone who has hidden behind the excuse 'I can't sing' since the onset of puberty.

1. Vocal disenfranchisement

THE PROBLEM

If any group of people is asked, 'How many of you cannot sing?' one in four will raise their hands to confess tone-deafness, no sense of pitch or some other musical deficiency.

When this quarter of the company are asked why they cannot sing, nearly all will say, 'Because someone told me.' And that 'someone' will inevitably have been a person who was in a position of authority over them or who was in close friendship or kinship with them.

One in four is an horrendous proportion of the population. But it is a specifically European, and more especially British, predicament. In other continents, the presumption is that everyone can sing. In some tribal societies singing, composing and teaching a song to others is part of the rite of initiation into manhood. But in Western Europe, the presumption that all can sing is displaced by the belief that some can and some cannot. Those who can't have all been told.

The fact must be stated straight away that there is actually a very small proportion of people who cannot replicate a melody in the right key — and some attention will be given to them later. Their difficulty is a physiological one which has to do with how hearing sound and making sound connect in their head.

For the others, the reason for the 'tunelessness' or 'tone-deafness' is psychological.

Yet to use the word *psychological* is to attach too strong or too technical a term to the condition. Perhaps it would be preferable, though less tidy, to say that for many people their memory of being told they could not sing has had such a cataclysmic effect on them that it prevents them from believing that their voices could ever get it right.

Memories have that effect on us.

One week at Iona Abbey, there was a seminar based on the biblical story of the call of Samuel (1 Samuel:1). The leader made the point, mentioned above, that the voices we hear when we are young reverberate in us throughout our lives, sometimes enabling or disabling us in particular activities.

The group – a very diverse mixture of academics, consultants, housewives and artisans – were asked to describe the voices which they personally heard echoing through the corridors of time into their present existence. It was a very revelatory moment, as one by one people recounted the voices and phrases that still belittled them.

One man said he kept hearing a particular person calling him a 'Jessie' because as a youth he had been slightly effeminate. An author said she still heard a teacher's voice calling her 'a proper little madam'. A doctor said that he was haunted by his grandmother's voice saying, 'You'll never be as good as your father.' And others recounted how they would be about to sketch a map to show a friend how to get from A to B when they would hear an art-master's voice proclaiming, 'You can't draw!' It became transparent that no matter how sophisticated, cultured, articulate or capable people are in their adult lives, the voices they heard in their childhood can still disable them.

It is exactly the same for those who believe they cannot sing because someone once told them so. Across the years the pronouncement of doom reverberates.

For those who have not had this experience, it is comparable to hearing as a child that your grandparent or favourite aunt or uncle has died. Many people are able in their mind's eye to replicate exactly where they were, what they were doing, what time of day it was when someone gave them the news that a dear relative or close friend had died.

It is as if the memory takes an audio-visual recording of the incident which can be action-replayed at the drop of a hat. Something inside instinctively informs us that from this moment on our life will be different. The person who has been so much a part of us is no longer. We are bereft of someone who was vital to us and we are helplessly diminished.

This is exactly what happens when we are told we can't sing. The memory registers the moment. Somewhere deep inside the cataclysmic news begins its debilitating impact. The very thing we presumed to be alive – our singing voice – is actually moribund. Its death certificate has been validated by someone in authority who knows about these things, or by someone we love whose word we believe.

In all probability, at the moment when our singing caused our critics to make such comments, we may have been temporarily out of key, or droning tunelessly. And this could have been to do with our having a cold, or an ear infection, or going through adolescence, a time when our voice naturally changes.

But not being in a position of knowing the truth, or of being able to argue against the authority making the pronouncement, we accept the judgement and begin a life sentence of vocal disenfranchisement. Thereafter we are likely to continue to sing quietly and without confidence, often in tune and in time, but steadfastly believing that we are getting it wrong.

I remember standing next to a Roman Catholic priest during a liturgy in Northern Ireland. After the service, I said to the priest, 'It's good to stand beside a man who actually sings at mass.'

'Oh, I don't sing,' replied the priest, 'I can't. I'm tone deaf.'

'Not at all!' I protested. 'There were three hymns plus a psalm and the Sanctus and you sang every one of them.'

'You're just saying that to make me feel good,' he said.

'Listen, I'm not making out that you're Pavarotti. But I want you to know that you sang all through mass and that you sang in tune.'

But still he would not believe it.

There is a remedy for such people, for the vast majority of those who believe they can't sing, and it does not involve a long course of psychoanalysis or training in vocal technique. It has to do with renaming and decision-making. But before elaborating on these, here are a few other testimonies from the self-confessed tone deaf.

FOUR TESTIMONIES

Andrew's story

Andrew was in his sixties. He had worked in religious broadcasting most of his life.

At an Advent carol service one year he was asked if he had enjoyed the service.

'All except the singing,' he replied.

'What was wrong with the singing?' asked his friend.

'I can't sing,' he responded.

'Who told you?' his friend enquired.

'Miss Brown.'

'When was this?'

'Oh it was a while ago.' And then he recounted with great accuracy the precise moment:

'We were in the music class. It was a Friday afternoon. I was sitting at the back beside Alex MacAskill. We were singing a folk song, a border ballad. I think it was *March, March, Ettrick and Teviotdale*. Suddenly Miss Brown stopped playing the piano and began to speak directly to me.

'She said, "Andrew Sloan, would you just mime please. You're putting the other boys off." So I've never sung from that day to this.'

Asked when exactly that had happened, Andrew replied, 'I remember that the windows in the music room were painted round the edges of the glass. And I remember it had big dark curtains. So it must have been during the blackout in the war. Maybe about 1940–41.'

'And what age was Miss Brown?'

'She'd probably have been about 26. All the older male teachers had got called up to the army.'

His friend then pointed out to Andrew that he, a man approaching seventy, was allowing his singing voice to be held ransom by a woman who was less than half his age.

He had never looked at it that way.

Margaret's story

Margaret was at a weekend conference for her local church. There was a lot of singing over the three days and at the end of the conference she came up to say how this was the first time she had sung for thirty years. She was asked the reason why.

'When I was a wee girl,' she replied, 'I used to sing all the time. Then one day my mother said to me, "Margaret, God wants you to praise him with your heart and your voice, and I think he'd be better pleased if you just used your heart." That was the day when I stopped singing.'

Denis's story

Denis is a clergyman who felt very embarrassed about his voice. He hated officiating at weddings or funerals when few people were keen to sing, and he had to give a lead. Asked when he first felt awkward about his voice, he gave this reply:

'When I was 18, I began to go out with a girl who went to music college. I had a great crush on her and would do anything to be in her company, including going to her church, which was not what you might call a sanctuary of my choice.

'One Monday after we had been at church the previous evening she asked if I would do her a favour. When I asked her what it was, she said, 'If we go back to church together, would you mind not singing so loudly. It isn't very tuneful.'

'So, because she knew something about music and I didn't, I decided that she could sing and I couldn't.'

Sarah's story

But most startling of all is the testimony of Sarah Farley. Sarah was in her early sixties and attending a conference at Iona Abbey.

At this conference, Alison Adam, one of the Wild Goose Resource Team had been asked to introduce some music from a new song collection entitled *Love and Anger*. Alison accordingly went around the participants and chose twelve people whose musical abilities were not known to her. As it happened, a quarter could read music, but as is her wont she had the whole group singing four songs in four-part harmony before the first rehearsal was over.

The scratch choir eventually presented the songs to the conference and were warmly congratulated. They had made a good sound.

After it was over, Sarah Farley who had been singing soprano came to talk to Alison. She said, 'Alison, I can't believe it. This is the first time I've sung in fifty years, and I was singing soprano in the front row of a choir!'

When Alison asked her why that was, she gave her testimony:

'When I was twelve, I went to an all girls' school. Early on in the first year, we were sitting in the music class and the teacher said that she thought someone was singing off key. So she went round the class girl by girl until she came to me. She made me sing in front of everyone and then told me that I shouldn't sing in class again, just mime. And from that day to this I've never sung.'

The sequel to this tale is that when I was telling Sarah's story at a conference a year later, a young woman shouted from the audience, 'He's telling the truth.'

All ears were attentive as she continued, 'He's telling the truth. Sarah Farley is my mother. When we were children, we never heard her sing. She always told us that she couldn't.'

Dozens of similar stories could be told, all of which have the common denominator of a person in authority or a loved friend or relative telling the individual at a young or transitional stage in their life that they couldn't sing.

Because the accused could not argue against the criticism, they believed it. Because no one has persuasively contradicted the opinion, they believe it twenty or thirty or fifty years later.

What is the remedy?

THE REMEDY

Renaming and decision-making are the essential means to recovery.

Renaming

The phrase 'give a dog a bad name and it will stick to it' applies as much to vocal confidence as to canine obedience.

When people are told they can't sing, they feel that there is a label round their neck or a mark on their file indicating a permanent disability.

What they need to do is move from that negative assumption or label to a positive one. And this transition is a very biblical thing, because God is in the renaming business. Abram becomes Abraham, Sarai becomes Sarah – and this because the new name indicates a more positive state of being. It comes when they agree to be liberated by God from the sterility which surrounds them.

In the Gospels, Jesus does the same thing. He takes Simon who is fully aware of his unreliability and, flying in the face of common sense, decides to call him Peter – the Rock, on which the Church is to be built. When confronted with a disfigured woman who would be called mad or diseased or something more impolite by her fellow citizens and their children, Jesus brings her into the middle of the synagogue and calls her 'a daughter of Abraham'.

Renaming is part of God's business. God delights to get rid of the rumours, nicknames and debilitating labels of the past. God identifies the potential rather than bemoaning the problematic.

So, whenever people refer to themselves as being tone deaf

or tuneless, somehow they have to discover that theirs is a voice in the making, or a voice in the waiting. They have to realise that they are expected by God and the people of God to sing, irrespective of what they have heard or believed about themselves in the past.

And the people responsible for changing the name and the expectation are those who in the leadership of music and worship decide either to encourage all of God's people to praise their Maker with their voices, or who make it clear from their demeanour and conversation that they anticipate and desire only those who are musically 'gifted' to engage in song.

Church musicians, in God's name, have to rename all the self-confessed groaners as apprentice angels, and to believe that they will begin to sing.

Annette's story

The proof of the pudding can be found in the story of Annette, arguably one of the most vocally disadvantaged of women. Her voice wandered off and on pitch, and made a terrible rasping sound, no doubt aided and abetted by copious supplies of nicotine and a past history of alcoholism.

She attended a weekend conference for church musicians where it was put to her that she had the voice of an apprentice angel – something which she clearly doubted. But over the weekend she engaged in every seminar, tried songs she had never sung before, and began to exhibit a quiet self-confidence.

Three weeks later, Annette phoned the conference leader to

ask if he would come to her church one Friday to help a group of people to pray. She explained that many were struggling with poverty or addiction or emotional traumas and that Friday night was a safe evening for these folk in a safe place.

When the leader arrived, quite at sea as to what to do in a situation which was alien to him, he was met by Annette who informed him: 'You don't have to worry about the singing thing. They can all do it. I taught them the Russian *Kyrie* in three parts the way you taught me. I just said to them, "Listen, I have been told that I have the voice of an apprentice angel. And if I can make music, all of you can." '

She then took her friend into a room where everybody's face told of a history of sadness, marginalisation or abuse. And to his astonishment she began to get them to sing in three parts the Ortho-dox *Kyrie* cited earlier (p.30). He did not have to do much to enable them to pray. They were half way there, thanks to the efforts of a husky-throated woman who took on a new name for herself.

We develop by growing into the fullness of life God intends for us, not by repeating the limiting labels of the past which dimin-ish us.

Decision-making

The other part of the remedy has to do with decision-making.

The conversation in which Andrew Sloan told his friend how Miss Brown had pronounced the death sentence on his voice during a wartime music class led the friend to say to Andrew, 'For you to sing you have to make a choice, a theological choice. Who is bigger? Miss Brown, who was less than half your age when she told you that you couldn't sing, or God, who says to you, "Sing me a new song"?'

For it is perfectly possible that the Miss Browns of the world were ignorant as regards male teenage voice development. It is possible that the Miss Browns were motivated in their comments more by a dislike of teenage boys than by discerning judgement about adolescent voices. It is also possible that the Miss Browns just got it wrong.

God, on the other hand, never asks people to do what they cannot. When God asks us to sing a new song, it is because God believes that we can.

Is it as simple as this?

Yes. It is as simple as this. The much more complex matter is for musicians to stop telling children and teenagers whose voices haven't matured or are temporarily dysfunctional that they can't sing. And it is even more difficult for musicians – in the face of their academic training and desire to demonstrate choral and vocal technique – to believe that simply by including everyone in the song, and by willing people to sing together, the groaners and the tuneless folk will find their voice.

It is something which must be done corporately. People who have been told in front of others that they can't sing have to be encouraged, in the presence of others, to sing. This does not imply singling them out for individual attention. It simply requires that they feel implicitly expected to be one *of* the crowd, rather than one *outside* it.

BUT WHAT ABOUT THE REAL GROANERS?

The small minority whose difficulty is not so much psychological as physiological present more of a problem. Among them there may be a very few people who, despite their love of music, will never be able to hold a tune. As with those who discover that they can't whistle though they'd like to, or can't be electricians because they are colour blind, such people simply have to live with that restriction, but should never be disenfranchised from the enjoyment of music. Indeed in some churches such people are the greatest encouragers.

But within the number of those who are physiologically unable to sing in tune there are some who will find the remedy when they are put in touch with their own voice.

Here are two case studies:

Grant's story

Grant was 19 when he joined our worship group. He was self-consciously tall and lanky. He had an innate sense of the theatrical, but a fairly dull voice. When he sang it was usually in a monotone, even when he sat in the middle of four basses who could all keep their line.

I decided to sit beside Grant when we were learning a song, and to teach the bass line to 'lah'. Using a technique which will be described in the second book, the degree to which my hand was raised or lowered imitated the pitch of the notes.

After a few weeks of doing this in close proximity to Grant, sitting beside him rather than in front of him, I noticed two things happening. The first was that he was beginning to differentiate between high notes and low notes. The second was that his head was going up and down as he followed my hand.

A few weeks later I revealed to his astonishment that he was actually singing the bass line, but that it only happened when his head physically moved up and down according to his perception of the notes as high or low. Now that he knew he could sing a line, he had to trust his voice to go up and down without his head moving at the same time.

Two years later, Grant was at drama college and I went to see him in a production in which he sang a solo – in perfect tune.

Angela's story

Angela was 37. She had come to an Easter retreat at which there was a lot of singing. She had heard my colleagues and me claim that everyone could sing, and she desperately wanted to, because underneath she believed it. But it wasn't working for her.

She told me her story. She had believed that she was tone deaf since a church organist had made that pronouncement when she was a child.

In her twenties she married a musician who promised that he would spend time enabling her to sing. He tried all he could, but it didn't work. Thereafter, when they were in company, if someone asked if they ever made music together, her husband would respond, 'Angela can't sing. Believe me. I've tried every trick I know.'

By the time we met, her marriage had ended, and her self-esteem was very low. But what intrigued me was that her voice – as distinct from Grant's – was naturally musical. When she spoke she used high and low registers, and this was intentional rather than haphazard.

We met in a room where no one else could hear us and, with some trepidation, I said that I'd like to hear her sing. To prevent any initial awkwardness I suggested that I would sing at the same time, and that we would sing the children's nursery rhyme *Twinkle, Twinkle Little Star*. It was not a very pleasant sound. There was no fluctuation, just a drone.

For reasons which I cannot explain, I asked if we might sing it again, but this time I would put my hand over one of her ears. There was a distinct difference. Not only did she approximate the pitch of the starting note, but her voice began to fluctuate.

I tried again with both her ears free, and then with one covered. It struck me that when one ear was covered she was more attuned to what was happening in her own voice, whereas when both ears were open she was only listening to me and could not connect with her own sounds.

I asked her if she had ever heard her own voice, if she knew inside what it sounded like. She said no. So I asked her to sing the same rhyme, and I put my hands over both her ears. Immediately the colour and inflection went and the drone came back. I asked her what she had heard.

'It sounded awful,' she said. 'It was a noise which seemed very far away.'

'That,' I said, 'is your voice. And it's like an orphaned child which needs to be loved by its mother. The more you listen to your voice, encourage your voice, become familiar with your voice, the better it will become.'

It was evident that something in her make-up had only let her hear what other people sang, and that both confirmed her own inability to sing a tune and alienated her further from hearing what was happening in her voice.

I suggested to her that she should sing along with the radio, television or CD player any songs which she particularly liked, but always with one ear covered so that she could hear the sound she was making and check it against the sound the performer was making. I suggested that she do the same thing, discreetly, in church, listening with the open ear to the congregation, and with the covered ear to herself. I met her a year later and she said things were beginning to come right.

It should be noted that whether the remedy involves changing self-perception, or making an existential choice, or watching visually whether a melody goes up or down, or trying to hear inwardly one's own voice and match it to the melody being sung by others, this takes time.

There is no instant remedy. There are no pills and there is no psychiatrist's chair. If it has taken someone thirty years to 'lose' their voice, it might take them three months or three years to find it. The important thing is to believe that it is possible.

God never asks people to do what they can't.

FOOTNOTE

What is true for individuals in this respect is true also for congregations. We discovered this when two of us spent some time attached to a church in an Urban Priority Area in Glasgow.

The congregational singing was dire. Worse still, several people in the congregation were keen to tell us that 'this is the church that can't sing'. Every Sunday they evidently stood up to prove it.

What had happened was that somewhere in the distant past, which no one could specifically identify, either a musician or a minister had let the congregation know that it did not sing well. The whole community, hearing this word from an 'authority', took it seriously as a pronouncement on its abilities, and from that time onwards became reticent to sing.

When we began to work in the church, we met a group of twelve people every Thursday evening, to look at the worship life of the congregation and to discern ways in which it could be enlivened.

Only one of these twelve people could read music; the rest all presumed that they couldn't sing. So we began each Thursday evening meeting with twenty minutes in which we simply sat and sang. We sang favourite hymns, children's hymns, and gradually introduced new songs which were going to be included in church services.

After four months, not only did this small group of twelve people sing confidently, but the whole congregation were singing better, because of the presence in it of twelve people who had begun to believe in their own voices.

The objective proof of improvement came when a woman who had left the church two years previously to live in the Scottish Highlands came back to visit her daughter and to attend morning worship. 'I couldn't believe my ears,' she said. 'The last time I went to that church, it was like a congregation of tailor's dummies. But last Sunday they sang like linties (thrushes).'

Here, again, it was not a matter of lecturing the people or employing any slick recuperative technique. It was simply changing their self-perception from the church that couldn't sing to the church that could, and allowing people to believe in their own voices.

2. The fallout from a performance culture

The previous chapter dealt with the psychological and physio-logical reasons why some people don't sing; this chapter deals more with cultural or sociological ones.

That we live in a performance culture is unquestionable. Television, more than radio, has made it so. We are used to infor-mation, serious or flippant, being communicated to us in an enter-taining way.

Gone are the days when people would listen to or watch a programme which included a sage ruminating on some issue of national significance for ten minutes without interruption. We now have interventions, changed camera angles, inserts or advertise-ments to save us, allegedly, from boredom. The medium, as Marshall McLuhan first stated, is the message. This is paralleled in the world of music where we are almost unconsciously entering an era very different from any Western civilisation has previously known.

Throughout the ages, from cave and tree dwellers onwards, people have sung sometimes for recreational purposes, sometimes to pass on information. And in all civilisations it has been clear that some people have been more talented in singing – as in dancing or drumming – than others. These people have been accorded places as minstrels, story-tellers, valued artistes whose presence at tribal or community gatherings added something special. And frequently they – as in European nations of all sizes – were patronised by the Church, the aristocracy or the government.

But these people were never seen as the sole purveyors of music. Just as the presumption in Afro-American societies is that everybody can dance, but some are better at it than others, so there was a belief in every European society that everyone could and would sing, but that some might have a particular talent to admire.

In every civilisation there has emerged a corpus of song reflecting the aspirations, the history and the culture of the people. Many such songs – in Asian, African, European and American societies – would be the property of the community to be sung by the whole community. Or they might be of a call and response, or verse and chorus, structure, whereby one person might sing the details while the others came in with an affirmative reply.

And there would be some songs which were properly the preserve of the gifted singers and musicians, to whom the majority of people would give encouragement by listening. We can detect such a variety of songs in the book of Psalms.

Psalm 13 is clearly a solo song to be performed by one individual:

How long, O Lord, will you quite forget me?
How long, O Lord, will you turn your face from me?

How long, O Lord, must I suffer in my soul?
How long, how long, O Lord?

Psalm 139, on the other hand, is clearly a community lament:

Beside the streams of Babylon
We hung our harps and wept
when we remembered...

If, however, we turn to Psalm 136, we find a litany of God's great acts which would be sung by a soloist with everyone joining in a response:

It is good to give thanks to the Lord,
FOR GOD'S LOVE ENDURES FOR EVER,
Give thanks to the God of gods,
GOD'S LOVE ENDURES FOR EVER.
Give thanks to the Lord of lords,
GOD'S LOVE ENDURES FOR EVER;
who alone does marvellous works –
GOD'S LOVE ENDURES FOR EVER.

A less obvious cooperative venture may be the well loved Psalm 121. Some commentators see this as a song sung by and to those who were about to go on a journey, perhaps through mountains which – for the Jews – were places of physical danger as well as divine presence. A solo voice begins and the community responds:

Lifting my eyes up to the hills,
where will I find my aid?
YOUR HELP COMES ONLY FROM THE LORD
WHO EARTH AND HEAVEN MADE.

Similar structures of chorus and verse or call and response songs
are prevalent in the musical literature of all nations. One of the
more mundane examples comes from England:

I'll sing you one o,
green grow the rushes o.
WHAT IS YOUR ONE O?
GREEN GROW THE RUSHES O.

Long narrative songs and sea shanties will often have less contin-
uous interchange, preferring to wait till the end of a substantial
statement when the chorus will affirm what has been said, and
through giving the soloist a rest will enable him or her to get the
next verse ready.

Here's to the maiden of bashful fifteen,
now to the widow of fifty;
here's to the flounting extravagant queen,
and here's to the housewife that's thrifty.

Let the toast pass, drink to the lass,
I warrant she'll prove an excuse for the glass.
LET THE TOAST PASS, DRINK TO THE LASS,
I WARRANT SHE'LL PROVE AN EXCUSE FOR THE GLASS.

This variety of community songs, solo or performance songs, and interactive songs has been constant throughout the ages. And it has been the expectation of most popular performers, be they mediaeval minstrels, troubadours, balladeers, Victorian music hall performers, parlour ditty writers, or 1960s' folk and rock stars, that their audiences would be able to sing at least the choruses of most of their repertoire. So, if Bob Dylan appeared on stage anywhere in the English-speaking world in the '60s and began *Hey Mr Tambourine Man*, he would expect the audience to join with him at every chorus in the exact same way as the diva chosen to sing *Rule Britannia* at the Last Night of the Proms expects everyone to sing the chorus with her.

When in the 1960s I travelled on a school coach from Kilmarnock to Edinburgh to watch Scotland thrash the All Blacks at Murrayfield rugby stadium, the whole busload of testosterone-filled teenagers would sing all the way there and cry all the way back (Scotland seldom won).

The songs we sang going to the match were a diverse selection of 60s' hits, Gilbert and Sullivan arias and choruses, extracts from Britten's cantata *St Nicholas* and rugby songs of a somewhat coarser variety. The pop songs were picked up from radio, television and dance halls, the Gilbert and Sullivan and Britten had been taught for school performances, and the rugby songs came with puberty.

It is not so common these days to hear a crowd of boys singing such a variety of songs together. This is partly because singing is taught less in schools, and partly because the prevailing commercial music culture has moved from one of mimicking and participation to one in which the audience listens more, watches the music video or dances.

In 1999 the Rolling Stones on their British comeback tour were greeted by veteran and new enthusiasts who roared the choruses of *Jumping Jack Flash* or *Can't Get No Satisfaction*, because these songs can be sung by most voices and are constructed in a verse and chorus pattern. Present-day popular songs do not usually have such a predictable structure.

As mentioned above, the commercial music scene is now very diverse, but there is a common strand in much of it – namely that it is geared towards performance rather than participation. Acid rock, rap and techno funk are genres which do not easily allow teenage voices to combine in emulation of their video screen heroes.

In the West we are going into uncharted territory where music is increasingly seen as something which is the preserve of gifted individuals whom others are expected to listen to and admire. The more this aspect of musical culture prevails, the less will ordinary people perceive that it is their prerogative to sing and participate in communal music-making. Therefore when the Church invites people to sing hymns, it is doing something profoundly counter-cultural. It is both presuming that all can sing, and providing material specifically written so that the whole community can participate.

But the Church is not removed from the acids as well as the advantages of modernity. In order that all the people of God can be summoned to song, the Church has to ensure that it does not, in the way of the world, get performance and participation mixed up. In this respect, it would be salutory to enquire of church musicians what proportion of their time is spent preparing to engage the whole congregation in song over against the time spent in honing their own instrumental or vocal skills.

Some time ago I visited one of the 'growth' churches in Michigan. It was a huge auditorium which had four services per Sunday, each brimming with around fifteen hundred people. In the space of 65 minutes the congregation sang twice. The first time it was an old redemption hymn, the second time an easily repeatable chorus.

The other music came from a polished and well-paid pro-fessional quartet who must have taken up ten minutes of the service time with their rendering of contemporary worship songs. The line between entertainment and worship was perilously narrow.

It is interesting to note how the arrogance which the rebels of the 1970s and '80s discerned in traditional church musicians has often been transferred. Those who complained in a previous decade about the tyranny of the organ and the organist and the robed choir who 'don't want to do anything else but show off', are sometimes now in positions where, as leaders of worship bands or praise groups, they can offer an alternative.

But the same performance mentality seems often to transfer with the changed leadership. The congregation is confronted with a row of microphones behind which stand a row of instrumentalists and singers, one of whom may greet the assembly with the words,

'We're now going to move into a time of worship. We're going to sing three songs about the love of Jesus and we hope you'll all join in.'

If the people don't join in, it will not be because they can't sing or feel shy. It may be because the physical line-up of musicians reminds them of a concert where they listen rather than of a community where they join in. Or it may be because they haven't been taught the songs; or because the songs are from the performance rather than the participative category, and the musicians have not recognised that there is a difference.

Just as we would not expect a congregation to stand and sing *The Hallelujah Chorus* from Handel's *Messiah*, on the basis that this music is meant to be performed by a trained choir, so we should not expect an untaught congregation to join in a lengthy syncopated worship song if its writer intended it for solo performance, and recorded it as such on his or her latest CD.

We are creatures of our culture. We cannot undo that, nor can we fail to be influenced by trends in music as in literature. But the Church's musical mandate cannot be dictated by gifted artists or 'Christian' publishers with their eye on the profit margin. The voice of the performers will always be heard, and devotional CDs can always be purchased. But they are no substitute for the voice of the people actively praising their Maker.

3. Places and spaces

The place where people gather to worship God can help determine whether or not the song of the people is enabled or disabled. It is an architectural reality which is too rarely considered when halls or churches intended for communitarian use are built.

Here, briefly, are three aspects of this complex but important issue.

PUBLIC SPACE

The Victorian gents toilet at Rothesay Pier on the Island of Bute, the subterranean U-bahn stations in Frankfurt, the narthex of Iona Abbey and the crypt of St Mary's Cathedral, Sydney have little in common. As well as being built at different times and being used for different purposes, none of the constructions vaguely resembles the others.

Rothesay gents is a subterranean space with fairly limited use, and, unusually for a public convenience, is also a listed building. The walls are faced with glazed china brick and there is copper piping.

Frankfurt's subterranean U-bahn (like Washington DC metro)

stations have large arched ceilings at either end of which two tunnels disappear into the darkness. The surface is natural brick and there are no evident copper fitments.

The narthex of Iona Abbey is about four feet above the nave and is directly adjacent to it. Both form a long rectangular space with straight walls built from pink granite, and a plain wooden ceiling.

St Mary's Cathedral crypt is a sequence of arched bays resting on squat pillars. Much of the ceiling space is covered in ornate mosaic.

What these places have in common is that they are marvellous spaces in which to sing. The most inept of choirs can sound like professionals, and the most weedy soprano like Kiri te Kanawa.

Sadly – lamentably even – very few local churches have such an effect on a singing congregation. Sadder still, when churches are built, less and less thought seems to be given to what will enable this space to encourage good singing and to resonate with it.

The importance of good acoustics is something which mediaeval church builders knew a great deal about. Undoubtedly that is because the human voice had to lead the liturgy without any mechanical amplification. So the shape of the spaces and their surface materials were important if all were to hear what was being said or sung.

It is unlikely that many of this book's readers will ever have direct responsibility for designing a new church. But they may have some influence on those who are either planning such a building or redesigning an old one. In either case the following issues should be borne in mind. And for those who are nowhere near a building under construction or restructuring, the following issues may explain why some existing congregations don't sing well.

1. Physical shape

For singing to be enhanced and enabled, there has to be plenty of space. With vertical space, the sound goes up. A stone vaulted or a wooden barrelled roof or a high flat ceiling will help the sound to reverberate. Arches, side chapels, apses and bays will also help reverberation but may also create that echo effect which keeps a sound continuing even when the voice or instrument has stopped.

Horizontal space is less helpful, especially where there is a low ceiling and no hard surfaces to reflect sound.

Sound is also affected by the way people sit within the space. If everyone faces the front in a long nave at the end of which is an equally long and empty choir, the singing might be fulsome but seem flimsy to the congregation. This was the case in two 'Big Sings' which members of the Wild Goose Resource Group led in York Minster and Truro Cathedral. The spaces are magnificent, but the naves are so wide, the ceilings so high and the congregational seating plan so rigidly front-facing that the sound produced by the people had nothing to bounce off. It just seemed to fade in the distance.

Had people been able to face inwards on three or four sides, the sound would have been much more fulfilling for the singers.

That is one of the reasons why cathedral choirs sing in the more confined space in front of the altar and face each other. There are, of course, exceptions. The choir in Liverpool's Metropolitan Cathedral are outward facing – but they sing in a round building which is ideal for enhancing vocal sound. The choir in Westminster Cathedral sit in a crescent shape – but they are physically on a higher plane than the congregation and their sound reverberates nicely in the apse immediately around them.

2. Facing materials

Acoustic tiles are anathema.

That has to be said again: acoustic tiles are anathema, especially if they are installed en masse before the potential of the building to soak up or reflect sound has been fully explored.

Occasionally architects and their paymasters will stand in the empty shell of a newly constructed building, sense that there is the potential for considerable reverberation and decide to douse the brilliance by putting acoustic tiles on the ceiling. What they fail to consider is what the building will sound like when it is kitted out with seats and other furnishings, is carpeted and has a congregation *in situ*. The echo in an empty building is no guide to how it will sound when full, for the simple reason that human bodies soak up two thirds of the sound directed at them.

Yet again, acoustic tiles are anathema to good congregational singing. The best surfaces are stone, brick, glass, wood and tile. Carpets are also anathema. Our North American publishers,

GIA of Chicago, once produced a lapel badge which read CARPET BEDROOMS NOT CHURCHES!

Never has such a badge been more needed.

To discover what carpets do to sound, take a glass of water and pour it on the carpet. The rate at which it soaks up the water is comparable to the way in which it soaks up sound.

Porous surfaces – such as carpet, carpet tiles, curtains, cushions, cork panels, etc., all prevent sound from reverberating. They douse it. But sometimes in the alleged interests of aesthetics – or because someone has left a legacy – deep pile carpets are installed in the aisles, across the choir, under the pews. Every inch of carpet soaks up the sound and thereby diminishes people's ability to hear the sound they are making in praise of their Maker.

I was once asked to go to a church in Fife to introduce a new collection of congregational songs. The church had recently benefited from the sale of a redundant building and with this money the whole downstairs area had been covered in blue carpet from wall to wall. To decorate the building further, large swathes of blue thick cotton curtain adorned the walls.

Around two hundred people came. The first song was well known. But during the first verse, although people were singing with gusto, there was hardly enough sound produced to suggest that they were exercising their vocal cords. The only remedy was for everyone to sit at the back of the church under the gallery and use the ceiling as a resonator so that people could hear each other's voices.

Perhaps the worst building in my experience is the Roman Catholic cathedral at Paramatta near Sydney, Australia. In the worthy tradition of post Vatican II architecture the congregation is gathered round the altar rather than seated facing it.

It should be a very reverberant space. But it is severely handicapped by a low ceiling, acoustic tiles and carpeting. On one occasion when there was an assembly of around four hundred singers from throughout the diocese, the acoustic was as reverberant as that provided by a wet canvas marquee. Most unfortunate were three choirs who, although they stood on the carpeted altar steps barely fifteen feet from a grand piano, were unable to hear the accompaniment simply because of the inept features of the building.

SEATING AND SOUND

It was noted above that if a congregation sits in a long building, all facing the front, they may be unable to feel fulfilled in their singing.

Because congregational song is a corporate activity, people need to feel connected, and having them all face one direction does not encourage that sense of connectedness. It is interesting that both the Protestant reformers of the 16th century and the Vatican Council in the 20th century came to the same conclusion – that people must sense and acknowledge each other's presence in order to be a community.

That said, there are some configurations which are not helpful. Where a choir stands up for every hymn and arrays itself across the chancel, facing the congregation, it can be a forbidding sight which sends the subconscious message through the building: 'They are the ones who sing, the congregation just makes a noise in the background.'

Equally intimidating can be a row of microphones behind which stand the praise band and vocalists. Not only does it remind people of a stage, with all the undertones of audience and entertainment, but it gives the impression that congregational song needs amplification, which it properly does not.

In an Anglican church in Northumberland, the leader of the music group was keen to show a respected musician the layout for Sunday morning. The place where the music group located itself was distinguished by a clutter of steel rods and cables to the right hand side of the altar and the music leader was hoping for advice on what sound amplification equipment would help the group to do their job better.

The 'external adviser', to the astonishment of the leader, suggested that perhaps on the following Sunday the group might occupy an unused area in the centre of the south aisle and – worse than that – might use acoustic instruments and let the stone and plaster aisle walls act as natural resonators.

The effect on the congregation was transforming. For the first time since the praise band had been 'leading', the congregation began to sing! The awkward thing was dealing with the dented egos of the church musicians who, though avowing their keenness to enable the congregational song, felt sidelined because the newly discovered bandstand was not so visible as their former location.

People who lead choirs should also think about where they are situated.

There is no reason to believe that the best place for a choir in any given building is at the front. If the choir has no straight wall immediately behind them or arched roof immediately over them, there may be nothing to help their voices blend.

Put them at the back of the church, under the gallery, or put them in a side aisle with a marble floor under them and a stone wall behind, and their sound will improve dramatically, soon followed by their self-confidence when they hear how they are singing.

In one Glasgow church the choir in its heyday sat at the very back of the gallery, behind the organ console. When, thirty years after the choir's demise, the church appointed a new musician, she decided to have the newly formed singing group sit downstairs in two pews immediately behind the congregation. It meant they would not be 'seen', but it resulted in their voices blending in a way which could have happened nowhere else in the church.

It is much preferable to resite a choir or group than to invest in electronic voice enhancers or microphones. Human voices need good space in which to reverberate, in the same way that piano strings need a good metal frame, or violin strings need a good wooden case to amplify, mix and mellow the tones that are created when the strings are struck or played. When you put voices through microphones, you do not allow the space to do the blending; it is the sound mixer which does it, and the effect is never as natural or resonant.

Finally, a word about how the congregation seats itself in the building.

If people sit more than four feet away from each other, they won't sing in case they are heard. If they sit less than four feet away from each other, they will sing because they hear others singing. It is as simple as that, and has to be taken seriously.

A new organ, a new praise group, a bigger choir will not make a congregation sing any better if they are encouraged to sit all over a church, preserving the maximum of private space around themselves. Public worship is not private devotion, and ministers and musicians have to be clear that encouraging this kind of individualism is the enemy of corporate liturgy and community singing.

When people are encouraged to sit close to each other and sing together, they will make a good sound even in the dullest of buildings; but where, amidst carpets, sound systems and acoustic tiles, they loll in splendid isolation in their favoured pew, they simply cannot fufil the mandate to praise their Maker as the community God has chosen.

4. Bad leadership

The last section alluded to the possibility that if a congregation does not sing well, it might be as much to do with the leadership as the membership.

After all, if a comedian discovers that an audience is not laughing at his jokes, he might blame it on the seats being uncomfortable, or on the temperature of the building being too high or too low; he might think to himself that they are just a weird bunch of humourless pedants. But he might also ask whether his jokes are not funny and whether that is why people are not laughing.

Are those of us who are leaders in worship willing to be as honest?

We all know what bad leadership is like:

– the guitarists who arrive when most people are already gathered, then strut about self-importantly tuning up, testing the microphones, making gruff comments to each other, all in full view of the congregation. Then, making a show of forced piety, they tell the watching assembly how 'wonderful it is to be with you in God's presence'.

– the organist who never practises the hymns, but who insists on playing them very loudly whether the text is about sorrow and death or joy and resurrection, and who refuses to play contemporary percussive songs on the piano, believing that all the best music was written before Bach died and that pipe organs were decreed by divine dictat.

   – the worship leader who patronises the choir and musicians by telling them how good 'that' was, even when 'that' was awful, but who would never dream of saying an encouraging word to the congregation.

   – the choir whose altos and sopranos amble in with huge handbags which one presumes must contain secret love letters, bank statements and hereditary jewellery, and who take deep offence when they are asked to vacate their sacred space for one service so that children can present a play.

   – the soloist who has spent more time in front of the mirror than on his/her knees and who, as if cantoring or singing a solo were insufficient, insists on bawling his/her guts out during every congregational song, just in case people forget that s/he is there.

   Yes, we all know what bad, fussy, self-important, disparaging leadership of music can be like. So why does it happen? As often as not, it is because the musicians see themselves as apart from the congregation rather than a part of it.

   This was strikingly evident in a D. Min. project for pastors studying at Bangor Theological Seminary, Maine. Fourteen of them had been asked to do a musical profile of their congregations. Twelve of the profiles were very staid, two were very adventurous. By whim rather than calculation, I asked the pastors (who came from Reformed, Episcopal and Catholic churches) which of their musicians went to coffee hour after mass or morning service.

In twelve of the churches, the musicians appeared ten minutes before starting time, lifted a hymn list from the vestry table, played the service and afterwards changed from their organ slippers to their driving shoes and motored home.

But in the other two, the musicians hung around. They got to know the congregation by name. They discovered which teenagers were at college and would only be home in the holidays; they found out when musicians in the armed forces were likely to be on home leave; they made it their business to ask who – even in their distant youth – had played an instrument or sung, and they moulded a music programme round the potentials and availability of the people. Furthermore, by endearing themselves to the congregation as interested musicians who took their role seriously, they were able to introduce new material without complaint and to affirm the congregation's song.

Church musicians have to be team players. Prima donnas are best in the concert hall.

SECTION THREE

The ambiguity of communication

When we deal with liturgical music, we are – in the main – dealing with a combination of words and sounds in hymns, psalms, anthems, chants and a range of other material. Historically, although the Church has found a place for instrumental music at different times within different denominations, most church music has to do with the association of a text with a tune.

It has to be said that, from the beginning, this combination has caused concord and conflict in equal proportions.

We can observe this in our contemporary context. We may know choirs which face the congregation and refuse to sing if the congregational item comes from a book which the choristers do not favour. We may know of congregations almost torn apart not by theology, but by musical taste. We may ourselves have experienced the curious sense of upset when a text we have long sung to a familiar tune is suddenly married to a melody which – in our humble but biased opinion – is totally inadequate.

But this is not 'from the beginning'. So let us look at the long-term context and go back almost three thousand years, to the time before the psalms were collected and published in one volume, to the days when the Hebrews were about to have the Ark of the Covenant returned to them. The excitement was universal. Not only were commoners and lay people overjoyed, David the king could not contain his delight. So he voluntarily took part in a musical procession in which he publicly and energetically danced before the Ark. His wife, Michal, a precursor of Queen Victoria, was not amused. Her words, if not her face, made that evident:

What a glorious day for the king of Israel, when he made an exhibition of himself in the sight of his servant's slave girls as any vulgar clown might do.
(2 Samuel 6:20)

Elsewhere in the Old Testament, disdain at the offering of religious music comes not so much from an embarrassed wife as an angry husband. For God, the groom of his people Israel, lets his annoyance be known through the words of Amos:

Spare me the sound of your songs;
I shall not listen to the strumming of your instruments.
(Amos 5:23)

Evidently country and eastern is not God's preferred style.

And from the beginning of the recorded history of church music in Scotland, it is clear that not everyone delighted in what was being done.

Here, for instance, is a comment from the pen of a friend of Prince Henry, son of King David who gave Scotland the parish system. This complaint is probably over eight hundred years old:

Sometimes you will see them (the choristers) *with open mouths and their breath restrained as if they were expiring and not singing, and then by a ridiculous interruption of breath, they appear as if they are altogether silent.*

At other times they look like persons in agonies of death; then with a variety of gestures they impersonate comedians, their eyes roll, their shoulders are shaken upwards and downwards, their fingers move and dance to every note.

And this ridiculous behaviour is called religion; and when these things are frequently done, then God is said to be most honourably worshipped.

So the upset in the lowliest mission hall when the right hymn is played to the wrong tune has a pedigree which goes back through history from all the courts of earth to the chambers of heaven.

In the instance of God's disquiet, mentioned in Amos chapter 5, the reason for the malediction is evident: praise had become a substitute for justice. The worshippers had developed the unjustifiable notion that the louder they praised God, the more sophisticated their rituals, the more exotic their instrumentation –

You improvise on the lyre,
like David you invent musical instruments.
(Amos 6:5)

– then the more God would be pleased.

This was a manifestation of the psychological condition known as displacement activity. And God was not going to be fooled. Hence God's demand that they cease substituting worship for social action, and try instead to let 'justice flow down like a river, and righteousness like a never-failing torrent'. (Amos 5:24)

It is highly unlikely that the objections we raise or hear raised to the singing of a choir or a congregation are so deeply rooted in convictions about social policy. Few people would dare to suggest that the praise band in St Monica and St Gregory's should dispense with their expensive instruments and take up political banners or collecting cans instead.

So what is the cause of our contemporary unrest?

Let us move sideways a moment to an incident unconnected with music but involving liturgy.

During Advent 1999, I was invited by BBC television to preach in four broadcast services from different notable churches in England. On the second Sunday in Advent, the service was to be relayed from Manchester Cathedral. The producer suggested that I might keep in mind how, two days prior to the broadcast, a central section of Manchester's shopping area devastated earlier in the decade was to be reopened, and that reconciliation might therefore be a theme worth pondering.

On the morning, my sermon began:

'Apart from Glasgow, my two favourite cities in Britain are Manchester and Belfast. With Glasgow they have three things in common:

1. Each is considered to be out of the way, especially to people who live in the 'South',

2. Each is considered, by people who have never been there,

to be dirty and industrial.

3. Each has been scarred by sectarianism – Manchester in a physical way, through bombing, Glasgow in a psychological way, and Belfast in both these ways and also socially, politically and spiritually.

'I would also venture to say that while mainland Britain may have felt the pain and expense of sectarian violence, the people of Northern Ireland have also felt the pain and cost of suspicion and rejection by the mainland British.'

Shortly after this, there was a loud bang in the cathedral. I had no idea what had caused it, but – this being a live television broadcast – I decided to continue as if nothing had happened. What had happened was that a cable had been inadvertently dislodged and for around two minutes viewers had only vision and no sound coming through their televisions.

About a week later, I received a letter from a woman in England who wrote intelligibly and intelligently. It was 54 lines long, around 40 of which dealt in graphic detail with the woman's recollection of the London blitz of which she had some experience as a child.

After that long section she concluded,

I was about to put the television off, feeling so incensed by your comments...when you were cut off! Do not dismiss that as coincidence.... God needed to protect his loved ones in this country and the world over.

Her final injunction was to tell me that I should pray before I preach.

Looking at the perfectly cogent letter, one is led to wonder why an inordinate proportion is spent recounting scenes from the London blitz which was never mentioned in the sermon; and why there was the automatic assumption that I never communed with my Maker before opening my mouth. (Whether or not God commanded that the sound cable be disconnected is for the BBC to decide.)

One possible answer is that I reminded the viewer of someone she had no time for and therefore fell prey to the opprobrium stored up for my lookalike.

More likely is the possibility that the word 'bomb' produced such a profoundly emotive resonance in the woman's mind, due to tragic unforgettable memories of the Second World War, that in the accidental two-minute silence, all these, triggered off by one word, came flooding back and she took exception to someone who wasn't conceived in the blitz daring to pontificate about it.

Each of us, usually in less dramatic circumstances, will have experience of what may be called 'the ambiguity of communication'. What we say is not what the listener hears, or what we hear is not what the speaker has said. But something in the speaker's words has acted as a catalyst to focus the hearer's mind not on what is being discussed, but on something very deep within which may have no relationship to the subject being aired.

Communication is a complex thing. Words can never be guaranteed to have their intended effect simply because the speaker or writer does not know what is already in the head of the reader or listener. This has great bearing on church music and helps us to understand why some music is a source of blessing to one person but anathema to another.

We shall, for the moment, isolate musical sound from text and in each category discern three of the many resonances that make for ambiguity.

MUSICAL AMBIGUITY

When we hear a musical phrase...even if it is no more than a dozen notes, we become unconsciously affected by different aspects of sound which may produce in us positive, negative or ambivalent resonances.

Three of these aspects are:

the instrument or voice articulating the music
the style of the music
any discernible tune.

1. Instrument or voice

The sight, let alone the tone, of highland bagpipes fills some people with patriotic fervour and others with instant revulsion. The pipes don't have to play anything. They just have to appear and make their initial groans and gasps as the piper adjusts the tuning on the drones for people to be attracted or alienated.

It may be that the piper intends to play *Amazing Grace*,

which is perhaps the favourite hymn tune of the person who is feeling hostile, or possibly *The Skye Boat Song*, which is the least favourite folk tune of the bagpipe aficionado. The tune is not important, the instrument alone has been sufficient to attract or dismay.

The same might be said of how people in their fifties and older respond to the sight of guitars in church. Some immediately warm to the prospect of teenagers strumming away as they lead the singing of the congregation. Others, on seeing a guitar sitting against the chancel wall, may want to turn on their heel and seek an alternative sanctuary.

It could be that Segovia (reincarnated) was going to play his transcription of Bach's chaconne for unaccompanied violin. That would not matter. Internally a voice would be saying, 'There's a guitar there! You know what that means!' And the meaning would not be positive.

In such instances, people are reacting negatively or positively *not* to what is about to happen, but to what in the past has happened concerning the instrument in view.

The person who loves the bagpipes may be an exiled Scot, for whom that sound conveys a rather fanciful notion of home. (There are very few streets in Glasgow or Ullapool where pipes play morning to night. But there usually will be a piper – sometimes Canadian – playing near the Scott Monument in Edinburgh.)

For the person who is filled with loathing, it may be that the pipes remind him of his four years in Her Majesty's forces, and how twice, resplendent in heavy dress uniform on the hottest of

August days, while marching to the sound of pipes and drums, he collapsed with exhaustion in the middle of a ceremonial occasion.

The person who reacts positively at the sight of guitars in their church may either be remembering how dire the usual organist is who insists on accompanying syncopated choruses on the full swell with octave couplers and vibrato, or may be thinking back to the 1950s and to playing lead in a skiffle group which won a local talent contest.

The person who reacts negatively will undoubtedly be dealing with a different range of associations. It may be that their neighbour has a fourteen-year-old son who was given a second-hand Fender for Christmas and who has recently got a hold of an eighth-hand amplification system – 'and his bedroom is right next to mine, and honestly, Richard, I think he has the speakers facing into the wall so that his mother can't hear him in her bedroom, but I can hear him in mine...and I think it was Thursday night, or should I say Friday morning at half past one...'

One of the stunning developments in appreciation of serious music in the past decade has been the rise in popularity of opera, particularly operatic arias. Hitherto, for many people, opera was an elitist entertainment, with long rambling melodies, naive story-lines, and very expensive tickets. But now, Tamla Motown and Big Band enthusiasts alike find themselves responding positively to *Nessun Dorma* et al.

It is not because the music has changed. But it may be that the televisual images and voices of the genial, gregarious and over-sized Pavarotti and colleagues have endeared people to an art form for which all the previous associations were negative.

The instrument or the voice which articulates the music we listen to is the first of several factors which make for whether or not we like what we hear.

2. The style

Style or tone is the second and perhaps less distinct factor.

Some people turn on the radio, and they might never hear the complete melody or recognise the performer, but the fact that what is being broadcast is a programme of country and western music compels some to sit down and put their feet up, and others to change channel immediately. The same may be true of serious music devotees who turn on a classical music channel and react with interest or dismay to a sequence of rather torturous sounds played on what appears to be a string section in which every instrument is tuned at a different pitch.

In the case of the country and western programme, one listener is expressing an affection for easy and undemanding listening which reminds her of a favourite aunt's sitting room, while the other listener finds the voice of a choir master from the distant past ringing in his ear, denouncing country and western as 'trite, vulgar and rarely venturing beyond three chords on badly played guitars'.

In the case of the serious music broadcast, the enthusiast has realised that not all contemporary music is angular and unresolved, but that sometimes a composer works his or her argument through discord. The lack of harmonic or melodic cohesion is part of the composer's intention, and is sometimes an episode which has to be put in the context of the whole work. And the listener can date the dawning of his or her understanding to the time when a committed attempt was made to get inside Bartok's fourth String Quartet.

For the person who takes an instant dislike to the strangulated sounds, an entirely different set of bells are chiming. He has always liked the diatonic scale for melodies and finds contemporary harmony accessible only until Shostakovich. A single evening in the Royal Festival Hall listening to music from the pens of Stockhausen and Birtwhistle convinced him beyond a shadow of a doubt that the moderns and post-moderns simply do not understand musical aesthetics. So why bother to listen any longer to what is palpable rubbish?

3. The tune

Then we come to the tune itself, if there is a tune.

The bagpiper who plays *Amazing Grace* may have failed to tune his drones and may make a mess of embellishing the melody with grace-notes, but for the lady who is being photographed beside him, this is a moment of bliss, because *Amazing Grace* was the song that was sung when she took Jesus as her Lord at a Billy Graham rally in Seattle, Washington, twenty years ago.

Not so for the man who is scurrying in the opposite direction. Irrespective of his spiritual fervour or affection for bagpipe music, he is murmuring, 'I sang that damned tune every Monday morning when I was a boarder at Longthorne Boys School. I hated it then, and I hate it now.'

Tunes carry with them memories from the past – from where we were when we first heard this piece, of who was playing it, of whether or not it was a good experience. And all that experience from the past colours our appreciation in the present.

But, of course, not every tune we hear is one we have heard before. So, when we hear a melody for the first time, we often try to assimilate it into what we already know. We may even say to each other, 'That sounds very like…' And our affection for what it is like will be transferred to this new reality.

This sometimes allows tunes to cross cultures and be accepted in places entirely different from their point of origin. Two anecdotes bear witness to this.

Here is the first line of a longer tune which I once taught to an audience in the Midlands.

When people had (very quickly) picked up the tune, singing it to laa, they were asked where they thought it came from. Someone suggested Scotland. Then an older man with a strong Dublin accent stated confidently that it came from Ireland. When asked where precisely in Ireland it might have come from, he declared with equal confidence, 'It comes from around the Cork area.' And of that he was quite sure.

So it took him and the audience by surprise to be told that it actually came from South Korea.

Why had the audience picked it up so quickly, and why had one man so definitively attested to its origins? The reason is that the tune is in what is known as the pentatonic or five-note scale. That scale appears in the music of every continent, and enables some of the indigenous music of Africa or Asia or Latin America to be assimilated immediately by European ears.

When Professor Robert Davidson was moderator of the General Assembly of the Church of Scotland, he visited the congregation of the Three Self Church in China. On his return, he told me how he was astounded to have gone into this totally Chinese church in Beijing and discover that the tune to which the first psalm was sung was:

The tune is commonly known as *Kilmarnock*.

To compound Professor Davidson's amusement, I told of how around the same time I had been in Kilmarnock, a town in Ayrshire, and had led a congregation in the singing of this tune:

...which comes from China!

This transference of two very different tunes across continents happens simply because they are written on the same scale of five notes and therefore the inhabitants of Beijing and Kilmarnock can quickly associate the melody from far away with ones that are familiar to them.

Our ears are not neutral. They are conditioned by what they have heard in the past, and the associations that gather around certain instruments, styles and melodies affect for good or ill how we respond to new material we listen to.

It is because the early conditioning of individuals and their exposure to various styles of music will be de facto different that we discover diverse reactions to new music among otherwise like-minded people.

TEXTUAL AMBIGUITY

But because liturgical or church music is frequently associated with words, there is a further dimension of potential ambiguity in the way a hymn or song is perceived. Here we examine three of many aspects involved.

Any verbal communication comprises *words* using a particular *language* and addressing a particular theme or *context*. These three categories roughly correspond to instrument, style and melody noted above, but the text-related categories are more keenly ambiguous than their musical counterparts.

4. The word

When we sing the lines:

Make me a channel of your peace
or
Peace is flowing like a river

what are we referring to by the term 'peace'? It is only one word, but it is a word which appears in a thousand hymns, songs and choruses, and also occurs with regularity in the Bible. What does it mean?

Has it to do with a warm glow inside which is the result of sensing God's presence? Does it refer to the absence of interruption or doubt in our daily living? Or is it the longed-for cessation of violence in places where there is civil or international conflict?

Each of these (and many other) meanings of the word 'peace' may offer themselves within the different minds that constitute any worshipping assembly.

Or what about 'justice'?

This is a word which the psalms and the prophets use repeatedly. It also appears in the songs of the Church. But what precisely is its meaning? Does it refer to the punishment meted out to sinners at the end of time? Or the results of a fairly administered legal system? Or a change in the lending and debt-repayment schemes operated by the World Bank and the International Monetary Fund?

Or what about 'Zion', of which glorious things are spoken, to which the tribes of God go up and among whose children we may wish ourselves numbered.

Is Zion a locality of which Jews only should rightly be citizens? Or, as Isaiah suggests, is it a homeland for the people of all nations? Or does it refer to a heavenly reality from which we sense ourselves estranged?

In each of these cases, one word – only one word – offers the possibility of a wide range of understanding. And, inevitably, unless a person singing a hymn is made keenly aware of the intentions of the writer, whenever the words 'peace', 'justice' or 'Zion' appear, the interpretation or gloss put on them will be the result of previous experience and conditioning.

The person whose notion of 'peace' in a religious context is all about people being nice to each other in church may find offensive the suggestion that in a given hymn the writer's intention was to ask God to so influence political processes that interpersonal violence ceased in a particular situation of conflict.

A clear example of this is found in the way people respond to this text from Zimbabwe:

If you believe and I believe
and we together pray,
the Holy Spirit must come down
and set God's people free.

For some devoted users of that song, it has become a deep personal plea for an end to insensitive disturbance. These very people, who find immense 'peace' merely through singing the song repeatedly, find it hard to accept that it came originally from the struggle for Zimbabwean independence and that it was, to some extent, a national anthem for political liberation.

When we read words, we never do so neutrally, but colour their contemporary meaning through their past significance in our lives.

5. Language

When an organ begins to play the introduction to the hymn whose first line is *The day thou gavest, Lord, is ended* some people feel the welling-up of spiritual fervour, while others find the words a complete turn-off.

For the latter, the issue is that archaic language was not a feature of their early experience of church, and they do not understand why older people enter with enthusiasm into a Victorian time-warp every time hymns of this type are sung. Older people may interpret the reaction of their juniors as a lack of respect for the historic language of the Church ('If the King James Version was good enough for Jesus…').

In this instance, what has been intelligible since childhood for older singers is virtually a foreign language to those born after 1970 and that sociological fact should be appreciated before either group begins to condemn the sensitivities of the other.

A poignant example of how language sends ambiguous messages may be found in the original version of the text by Henry Francis Lyte

Praise the Lord, his glories show. Alleluia!

Everything seems intelligible to everybody until verse four is reached. Then we have the profound (or risqué) lines:

Strings and voice, hands and hearts, Alleluia!
In the concert bear your parts, Alleluia!

Older generations who immediately think of orchestral scores cannot understand the sniggering of younger generations and criticise their irreverence. But it is, at base, a simple indication that language is not a constant. Meanings and associations change, and what was clear for one generation can become obscure or ambiguous for another.

The issue of inclusivity has to be seen in this respect.

For a large number of men and women brought up in church circles prior to the 1970s, there was and still is nothing inherently wrong with a mixed congregation or even a women's meeting singing:

Name him, brothers, name him,
with love strong as death
or
O brother man, clasp to thy heart thy brother
or
Rise up, O men of God,
have done with lesser things.

'Of course it means men and women,' a chorus of mothers and grandmothers protest. 'We don't know what all the fuss is about.'

But these mothers and grandmothers may not have been reared in a society which has women's football teams, female members of parliament, female judges, a society in which terms like 'equal opportunities' and 'sexual harassment' are common parlance in the workplace, a society in which 'women's rights' are taken for granted.

For girls who have grown up since the 1980s, there is something dysfunctional about a church which ordains women, which allows women to chair its major commissions and committees, which might even allow for a theological understanding of the feminine in God, yet which in historic hymns, creeds and the language of written and extempore prayer relies heavily on male imagery and male categorisation for the people of God.

Why, one might ask, should a girl who has been brought up to believe that she is equal to a boy in the eyes of society, the law and God, surrender her gender identity when she crosses the threshold of a church?

Language is a powerful tool for controlling or liberating people, and in the song of the church it can include, exclude or antagonise. And debates about the rights and wrongs of certain terms may, despite their clear logic, still fail to bring harmony. In such cases it is not the logic of the argument which is right or wrong, it is the strength of different resonances reverberating in the minds of individuals. It is the language of the heart getting the upper hand over the language of the mind.

6. The subject or context

In 1998, the churches in Scotland cooperated to produce a volume of 150 songs entitled *Common Ground*. This was a singular venture in ecumenical liturgical engagement, possibly the first of its type in Europe.

The material in the book covered five centuries, but most of it came from contemporary writers and composers on all continents. It also reflected contemporary pastoral and theological concerns of the Church and, in the latter context, included four songs which alluded to the feminine or mothering characteristics of God and the Holy Spirit (who is represented by a female noun in Hebrew).

The book was promoted widely throughout Scotland and met with almost universal acclamation. But not in one lowland parish.

After an evening of singing new material (in which none of the songs dealing with the feminine in God was sung) the leader was confronted by a highly irate woman who maintained that she could not physically hold the book in her hand. When asked why, she blurted out, 'God is not a woman!'

The leader then asked if she was a Bible-believing Christian. The woman almost took exception to the question. Of course she was! Then the leader began to identify within the scriptures the allusions to the mothering qualities in God which had been picked up in the texts she clearly did not favour. But it was to no avail.

At one point the leader said, 'I think that even if I were to prove beyond question that the Bible refers to God in the feminine, you would still object to these hymns.' With that statement the woman was in total agreement.

What had caused her to be so deeply hostile to these texts that she felt she could not hold a book which contained them? There are two possible suggestions, neither of which has anything to do with theology or hymnody.

It might have been that just as some people shrink from biblical and liturgical language which emphasises the 'fatherhood' of God, on the basis that their own experience of a human father involved cruelty or abuse, the same might be true for this woman's experience of her mother.

If the relationship with either parent has been painful and demeaning, if the mere term 'father' or 'mother' is immediately evocative of unpleasant memories and associations, it is understandable that such a term might not be one the victim would want to associate with God.

There is, however, another possibility. It could have been that the woman was unable to have children, and that the pain of being unable to conceive was put in stark relief by the notion that God might be seen as a fertile mother in whose image we, her children, are made. If this were the case, the force of the angry woman's invective is quite understandable.

There are often mixed reactions to the kind of imagery we find in historical hymns such as:

Soldiers of Christ arise and put your armour on
or
Onward, Christian soldiers, marching as to war
or
I'm in the Lord's army.

From a biblical perspective, discipleship is sometimes described in military terms. St Paul urges his readers to 'put on the whole armour of God' and itemises what that armour consists of in the fight against the 'wiles of the devil'. That cannot be denied or argued away, and the defenders of such hymns have good biblical justification on their side.

The objectors, however, may also have a reasoned argument worth listening to. It may not simply be a political or ethical objection to the taking up of arms. Quite apart from pacifist arguments is the truth that the kind of warfare envisaged by St Paul in Ephesians 6 was of a very different variety from that waged today.

In the first century of the Christian era, most warfare relied on face to face combat where the warring forces would see those they were attacking and might have to grapple with them physically. This is a far cry from the kind of military operation behind, for example, the Gulf War, typified by sophisticated technology and a geographical distance of many miles between the opposing forces.

Additionally, we have to remember that far fewer people in the 21st century will know a soldier compared to those who grew up in the era of conscription when every second household had a son or daughter in the armed forces. Thus one might both say that the military metaphor for committed discipleship is justifiable in hymns because it has a biblical basis *and* at the same time concede that it might either fail to communicate or wrongly communicate its message to people who know little or nothing about conventional first-century warfare.

IN CONCLUSION

Our brief foray into how six aspects of liturgical words and music can have very different effects on worshippers vindicates the claim that communication is an extremely ambiguous exercise.

Both the speaker and the listener may be using terms which have an entirely different set of resonances in the other's mind and that can lead to the listener hearing what the speaker, writer or singer never intended. We do not bring simply our faith or our aesthetic appreciation to church music; we bring our childhood, our adolescence, our cultural and political sensitivities and all the associations and memories that they engender.

We are surely children of God, but we are equally creatures of our conditioning. To distinguish between the one and the other requires sometimes honesty, sometimes integrity and sometimes humble heroism.

Au revoir

Somewhere in the previous pages it was suggested that 'later' information would be given as to how exactly a congregation can be taught.

This being one the last pages of print, it is unlikely that the method will follow this epilogue unless it is sewn into the covers.

The truth is that you will have to purchase another book, or rather Part Two of this present volume.

We decided that rather than cram everything into one volume and run the risk of people skipping the theory in order to get on with the practice, we would separate the material into two volumes.

The second will deal specifically with how a congregation learns and, therefore, how it can be taught. It will also look at how the singing of congregations using traditional material can be improved.

Between now and then you might want to discuss the issues raised in this book with your choir, congregation, colleagues, fellow weight-watchers or those sitting near you in the dentist's waiting room.

Simply take a deep breath and say, 'What are the five main reasons why you sing?' And if somebody says 'I can't sing,' then you say'...

John L. Bell is a hymnwriter and composer based in Glasgow and working as part of the Wild Goose Resource Group of the Iona Community. With his colleagues he has produced 14 collections of original songs and anthems. These are published in North America and Australia as well as the UK, and translated selections are available in Norway, Sweden and Japan.

He lectures in liturgy and hymnody throughout Britain and abroad and in 1999 received an honorary Fellowship of the Royal School of Church Music.

The Iona Community

The Iona Community is an ecumenical Christian community, founded in 1938 by the late Lord MacLeod of Fuinary (the Revd George MacLeod DD) and committed to seeking new ways of living the Gospel in today's world. Gathered around the rebuilding of the ancient monastic buildings of Iona Abbey, but with its original inspiration in the poorest areas of Glasgow during the Depression, the Community has sought ever since the 'rebuilding of the common life', bringing together work and worship, prayer and politics, the sacred and the secular in ways that reflect its strongly incarnational theology.

The Community today is a movement of over 200 Members, around 1,500 Associate Members and about 700 Friends. The Members – women and men from many backgrounds and denominations, most in Britain, but some overseas – are committed to a rule of daily prayer and Bible reading, sharing and accounting for their use of time and money, regular meeting and action for justice and peace.

The Iona Community maintains three centres on Iona and Mull: Iona Abbey and the MacLeod Centre on Iona, and Camas Adventure Camp on the Ross of Mull. Its base is in Community House, Glasgow, where it also supports work with young people, the Wild Goose Resource and Worship Groups, a bimonthly magazine (Coracle) and a publishing house (Wild Goose Publications).

For further information on the Iona Community please contact:

The Iona Community
Pearce Institute,
840 Govan Road
Glasgow G51 3UU
Tel. 0141 445 4561; Fax 0141 445 4295
e-mail: ionacomm@gla.iona.org.uk
web: www.iona.org.uk